GRADES 6-8

LANGUAGE ARTS

Activities for the
Differentiated
Classroom

Gayle H. Gregory • Carolyn Chapman

CORWIN PRESS
Classroom

For information:

Corwin Press
A SAGE Publications Company
2455 Teller Road
Thousand Oaks, California 91320
CorwinPress.com

SAGE Publications, Ltd.
1 Oliver's Yard
55 City Road
London EC1Y 1SP
United Kingdom

SAGE Publications India Pvt. Ltd.
B 1/I 1 Mohan Cooperative
Industrial Area
Mathura Road, New Delhi
India 110 044

SAGE Publications Asia-Pacific Pvt. Ltd.
33 Pekin Street #02-01
Far East Square
Singapore 048763

Printed in the United States of America.

ISBN 978-1-4129-5343-6

This book is printed on acid-free paper.

08 09 10 11 12 10 9 8 7 6 5 4 3 2 1

Executive Editor: Kathleen Hex
Managing Developmental Editor: Christine Hood
Editorial Assistant: Anne O'Dell
Developmental Writer: Colleen Kessler
Developmental Editor: Karen Hall
Proofreader: Bette Darwin
Art Director: Anthony D. Paular
Cover Designer: Monique Hahn
Interior Production Artists: Scott Van Atta and Karine Hovsepian

Activities *for the* Differentiated Classroom

TABLE OF CONTENTS

Connections to Standards

This chart shows the national academic standards covered in each chapter.

READING	Standards are covered on pages
Read a wide range of print and nonprint texts to build an understanding of texts, of self, and of the cultures of the United States and the world; to acquire new information; to respond to the needs and demands of society and the workplace; and for personal fulfillment (including fiction and nonfiction, classic, and contemporary works).	12, 14, 42
Read a wide range of literature from many periods in many genres to build an understanding of the many dimensions (e.g., philosophical, ethical, aesthetic) of human experience.	9, 27, 34

WRITING	Standards are covered on pages
Apply a wide range of strategies to comprehend, interpret, evaluate, and appreciate texts. Draw on prior experience, interactions with other readers and writers, knowledge of word meaning and of other texts, word identification strategies, and understanding of textual features (e.g., sound-letter correspondence, sentence structure, context, graphics).	12, 24, 38, 66
Adjust the use of spoken, written, and visual language (e.g., conventions, style, vocabulary) to communicate effectively with a variety of audiences and for different purposes.	34, 75, 77, 86
Employ a wide range of strategies while writing, and use different writing process elements appropriately to communicate with different audiences for a variety of purposes.	45, 47, 55, 58, 73
Apply knowledge of language structure, language conventions (e.g., spelling and punctuation), media techniques, figurative language, and genre to create, critique, and discuss print and nonprint texts.	17, 53, 55, 62, 66, 69, 72, 76, 80

LANGUAGE CONVENTIONS	Standards are covered on pages
Conduct research on issues and interests by generating ideas and questions and posing problems. Gather, evaluate, and synthesize data from a variety of sources (e.g., print and nonprint texts, artifacts, people) to communicate discoveries in ways that suit the purpose and audience.	91
Use a variety of technological and informational resources (e.g., libraries, databases, computer networks, video) to gather and synthesize information and to create and communicate knowledge.	9
Develop an understanding of and respect for diversity in language use, patterns, and dialects across cultures, ethnic groups, geographic regions, and social roles.	50, 62, 75

LISTENING AND SPEAKING	Standards are covered on pages
Participate as knowledgeable, reflective, creative, and critical members of a variety of literacy communities.	38, 83
Use spoken, written, and visual language to accomplish a purpose (e.g., for learning, enjoyment, persuasion, and the exchange of information).	17, 42, 50, 65, 69, 70, 77, 81, 83, 91

Introduction

As a teacher who has adopted the differentiated philosophy, you design instruction to embrace the diversity of the unique students in your classroom and strategically select tools to build a classroom where all students can succeed. This requires careful planning and a very large toolkit! You must make decisions about what strategies and activities best meet the needs of the students in your classroom at that time. It is not a "one size fits all" approach.

When planning for differentiated instruction, include the steps described below. Refer to the planning model in *Differentiated Instructional Strategies: One Size Doesn't Fit All, Second Edition* (Gregory & Chapman, 2007) for more detailed information.

1. Establish standards, essential questions, and expectations for the lesson or unit.

2. Identify content, including facts, vocabulary, and essential skills.

3. Activate prior knowledge. Pre-assess students' levels of readiness for the learning and collect data on students' interests and attitudes about the topic.

4. Determine what students need to learn and how they will learn it. Plan various activities that complement the learning styles and readiness levels of all students in this particular class. Locate appropriate resources or materials for all levels of readiness.

5. Apply the strategies and adjust to meet students' varied needs.

6. Decide how you will assess students' knowledge. Consider providing choices for students to demonstrate what they know.

Differentiation does not mean always tiering every lesson for three levels of complexity or challenge. It *does* mean finding interesting, engaging, and appropriate ways to help students learn new concepts and skills. The practical activities in this book are designed to support your differentiated lesson plans. They are not pre-packaged units, but rather activities you can incorporate into your plan for meeting the unique needs of the students in your classroom *right now*. Use these activities as they fit into differentiated lessons or units you are planning. They might be used for total group lessons, to reinforce learning with individuals or small groups, to focus attention, to provide additional rehearsal opportunities, or to assess knowledge. Your differentiated toolkit should be brimming with engaging learning opportunities. Take out those tools and start building success for all your students!

Put It into Practice

Differentiation is a Philosophy

For years teachers planned "the lesson" and taught it to all students, knowing that some will get it and some will not. Faced with NCLB and armed with brain research, we now know that this method of lesson planning will not reach the needs of all students. Every student learns differently. In order to leave no child behind, we must teach differently.

Differentiation is a philosophy that enables teachers to plan strategically in order to reach the needs of the diverse learners in the classroom and to help them meet the standards. Supporters of differentiation as a philosophy believe:

- All students have areas of strength.

- All students have areas that need to be strengthened.

- Each student's brain is as unique as a fingerprint.

- It is never too late to learn.

- When beginning a new topic, students bring their prior knowledge base and experience to the new learning.

- Emotions, feelings, and attitudes affect learning.

- All students can learn.

- Students learn in different ways at different times.

The Differentiated Classroom

A differentiated classroom is one in which the teacher responds to the unique needs of the students in that room, at that time. Differentiated instruction provides a variety of options to successfully reach targeted standards. It meets learners where they are and offers challenging, appropriate options for them to achieve success.

Differentiating Content By differentiating content the standards are met while the needs of the particular students being taught are considered. The teacher strategically selects the information to teach and the best resources with which to teach it using different genres, leveling materials, using a variety of instructional materials, and providing choice.

Differentiating Assessment Tools Most teachers already differentiate assessment during and after the learning. However, it is equally important to assess what knowledge or interests students bring to the learning formally or informally.

Assessing student knowledge prior to the learning experience helps the teacher find out:

- What standards, objectives, concepts, skills the students already understand

- What further instruction and opportunities for mastery are needed

- What areas of interests and feelings will influence the topic under study

- How to establish flexible groups—total, alone, partner, small group

Differentiating Performance Tasks In a differentiated classroom, the teacher provides various opportunities and choices for the students to show what they've learned. Students use their strengths to show what they know through a reflection activity, a portfolio, or an authentic task.

Differentiating Instructional Strategies When teachers vary instructional strategies and activities, more students learn content and meet standards. By targeting diverse intelligences and learning styles, teachers can develop learning activities that help students work in their areas of strength as well as areas that still need strengthening.

Some of these instructional strategies include:

- Graphic organizers

- Cubing

- Role-playing

- Centers

- Choice boards

- Adjustable assignments

- Projects

- Academic contracts

When planning, teachers in the differentiated classroom focus on the standards, but also adjust and redesign the learning activities, tailoring them to the needs of the unique learners in each classroom. Teachers also consider how the brain operates and strive to use research-based, best practices to maximize student learning. Through differentiation we give students the opportunity to learn to their full potential. A differentiated classroom engages students and facilitates learning so all learners can succeed!

CHAPTER 1

Reading

Tall Tales

Standards

- Read a wide range of literature from many periods in many genres to build an understanding of the many dimensions (e.g., philosophical, ethical, aesthetic) of human experience.

- Use a variety of technological and informational resources (e.g., libraries, databases, computer networks, video) to gather and synthesize information and to create and communicate knowledge.

Strategies
Ability grouping

Multiple intelligences

Objective

Students will read, interpret, and evaluate tall tales.

Materials

Tall Tale Summary reproducible
collection of tall tales at different reading levels

In this activity, students will gain a deeper understanding and appreciation of tall tales as they read, evaluate, compare, summarize, and discuss stories of the genre.

1. Collect a variety of tall tales at different reading levels from your local library, or you might consider using online resources such as American Folklore at *www.americanfolklore.net*.

2. Invite students to share what they know about tall tales. Explain that a tall tale includes many exaggerations, whereas a regular tale does not. Write *Regular Tale* and *Tall Tale* on the board. Work with students to write a regular tale about an outdoor adventure. Then have students change it into a tall tale. For example: *I caught a fish; I caught a fish the size of Texas.* Encourage students to use exaggerated details to describe main characters, setting, and plot.

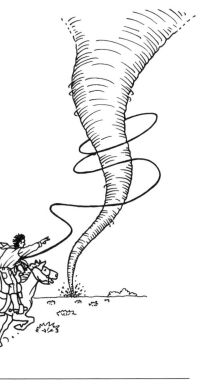

Tall Tale Summary Page 11

3. Divide the class into groups by reading ability, and distribute several tall tales to each group at the appropriate reading levels. Give each group a copy of the **Tall Tale Summary (page 11)** to complete for their tall tale.

4. Instruct groups to take turns reading their tall tales aloud as the rest of the group follows along. Encourage them to get into character as they read the story, using expressive voices and appropriate dialects.

5. Then have the group share their Tall Tale Summary sheet. Invite the class to add details and observations after each presentation.

6. Initiate a class discussion, inviting groups to share what they learned about tall tales. Ask students to identify some common attributes of tall tales, and write their suggestions on the board. For example: *Tall tales contain exaggerations. Tall tales include a lot of action and descriptive verbs and adjectives. Tall tales often include similes and metaphors. The main character must solve a problem. The main character is larger than life and has superhuman qualities. The plot is funny and impossible; the ending is surprising and unbelievable. The main character solves a problem, overcoming an obstacle or a villain.*

7. Invite groups to act out one of their tall tales for the class. Ask the audience to identify all the exaggerations in the story.

Ideas for More Differentiation

Develop a three-tiered activity, grouping students according to readiness levels. Give beginning mastery students the characteristics up front so they can find examples in their tall tales. For approaching mastery, have students complete the activity as written. For high-degree mastery students, provide a mixture of stories, some tall tales and some not, to compare and contrast.

Extend the Activity

Have students work independently or with a partner to write and illustrate their own tall tale to share with the class. Bind the stories together to make a class book.

Tall Tale Summary

Directions: Write about your tall tale below.

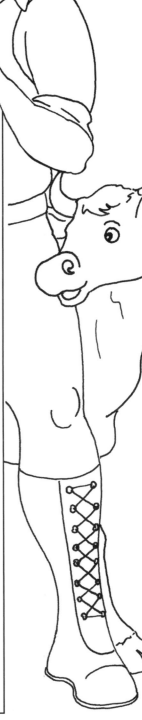

Title: _____

1. Name some exaggerations that take place in your tale.

_____

_____

2. List superhuman qualities your main character has.

_____

_____

3. What problem does your main character need to solve?

_____

_____

4. How does your main character solve the problem?

_____

_____

5. Describe some of the action using descriptive verbs and adjectives.

_____

_____

_____

Nonfiction Basketball

Standards

- Read a wide range of print and nonprint texts to build an understanding of texts, of self, and of the cultures of the United States and the world; to acquire new information; to respond to the needs and demands of society and the workplace; and for personal fulfillment (including fiction and nonfiction, classic, and contemporary works).

- Apply a wide range of strategies to comprehend, interpret, evaluate, and appreciate texts. Draw on prior experience, interactions with other readers and writers, knowledge of word meaning and of other texts, word identification strategies, and understanding of textual features (e.g., sound-letter correspondence, sentence structure, context, graphics).

Objective

Students will read and review factual information from textbooks as they play an indoor basketball game.

Materials

sets of science or social studies textbooks
index cards
foam basketball
toy basketball hoop or empty trashcan

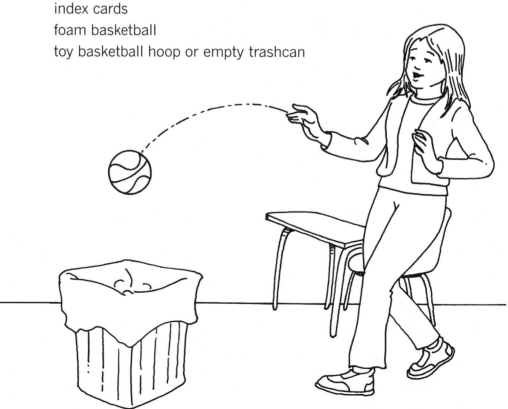

In this activity, students "jump for joy" as they incorporate an indoor game of basketball with reading and reviewing information from textbooks across the curriculum. It is also a great opportunity for inter-departmental cooperation and for students to discover that reading is an integral part of all subject areas.

1. In advance, borrow a set of grade-level science or social studies textbooks, and find out from those teachers what topics students are currently studying in class. Also get a foam basketball, and set up a toy basketball hoop (or use a trashcan).

2. Divide the class into two equal teams, and assign each team the same section of science or social studies to read in a given amount of time (e.g., 20 minutes). Tell students to write at least ten questions and answers about the text on separate index cards.

3. Invite teams to test each other's knowledge in a game of indoor basketball. Have them follow these directions:
   - A player on the opposing team asks the first player a question.
   - If the question is answered correctly, the team is awarded a point and the player that answered correctly can try to shoot the ball for an additional point.
   - If the question is answered incorrectly, the person who asked the question gets to shoot for a point.
   - If the answer provided on the card is incorrect, that team loses a point. If the opposing team challenges the answer and they are correct, their team loses a point.
   - Rotate players and continue playing with students taking turns asking and answering questions.
   - Points may be deducted for disruptive behavior.
   - The team with the most points at the end of the game wins.

Ideas for More Differentiation

- Provide a list of vocabulary words and terms for students to include in their questions. You might also assign partners to students who feel uncomfortable answering questions by themselves.

- For a more advanced game, have students write both a regular and more challenging question on each card, and award two points for answering the more difficult questions correctly.

Character Analysis

Strategies

Graphic organizer

Multiple intelligences

Standard
Read a wide range of print and nonprint texts to build an understanding of texts, of self, and of the cultures of the United States and the world; to acquire new information; to respond to the needs and demands of society and the workplace; and for personal fulfillment (including fiction and nonfiction, classic, and contemporary works).

Objective
Students will analyze and compare literary characters by completing visual outlines.

Materials
Character Analysis reproducible
current class novel or a selection of books
colored pencils or markers

Characters come alive for readers when they develop a deeper understanding of a protagonist's or antagonist's motivations and external influences through character analysis. A successful character analysis requires students to infer abstract traits and values from literal details given in the story. In this activity, students analyze characters from a novel by creating figurative drawings with descriptive details about who they are, how they react to others, and how they evolve in the story.

1. Give students a copy of the **Character Analysis reproducible (page 16)**. Explain that they will be using the outline to analyze a character in the novel they are currently reading (either a current class novel or novels that students are reading independently).

2. Draw a copy of the body outline on the board, or use a transparency of the reproducible. Demonstrate how to complete the outline by using a character from an novel read earlier in class or from a well-known story (such as the Harry Potter series). Invite volunteers to write responses in the outline.

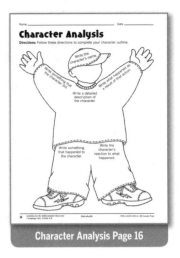

Character Analysis Page 16

3. Instruct students to complete their own outline about a character from a novel. They can focus on the most recently read chapter or refer to all of the chapters read thus far. Encourage students to skim through their book to review important details and find examples to write in their outline. Have them identify and analyze only the most important traits and actions of their character.

4. After they complete their outlines, pair up students to share and compare their work. Then have a class discussion, inviting students to share their results.

Ideas for More Differentiation

- Suggest that English Language Learners draw and label pictures instead of writing sentences for their answers. Encourage them to label their pictures in both English and their primary language. They can also work with an English-speaking partner.

- Encourage students with a high degree of mastery to complete two outlines for a pair of characters that have many opposite traits, such as a protagonist and antagonist, or a real character and a fantasy character. Have them use a pair of paper outlines to create a two-sided paper doll or puppet of the two characters. They can then use the puppet to compare and contrast the two characters and retell the story to classmates or younger students.

Extend the Activity

Invite students to make life-sized outlines of the characters on butcher paper and cut out the shapes. Then have them keep a running character analysis, adding new information after they read each chapter.

Character Analysis

Directions: Follow these directions to complete your character outline.

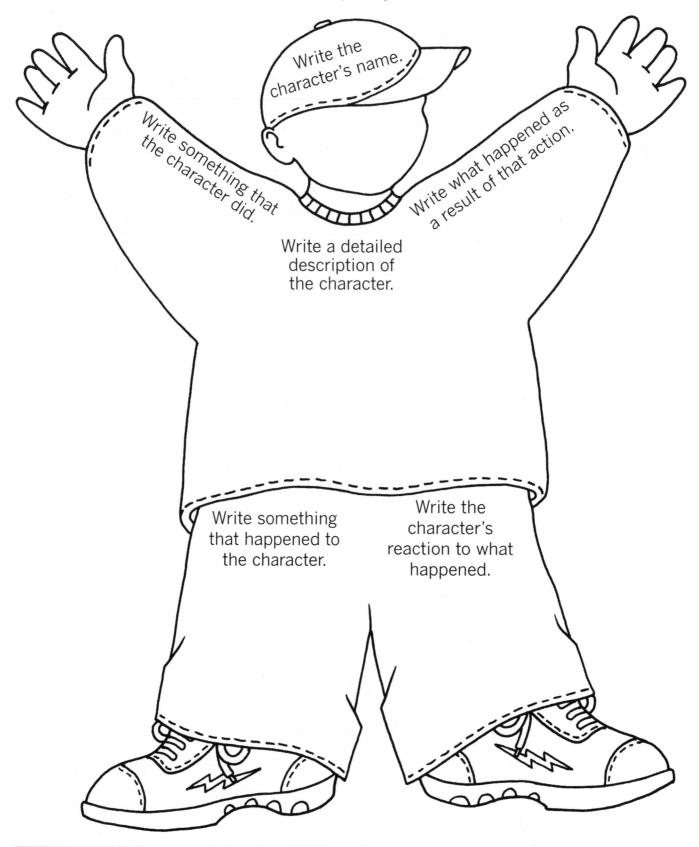

Write the character's name.

Write something that the character did.

Write what happened as a result of that action.

Write a detailed description of the character.

Write something that happened to the character.

Write the character's reaction to what happened.

Reproducible

Propaganda in the Media

Standards

- Apply knowledge of language structure, language conventions (e.g., spelling and punctuation), media techniques, figurative language, and genre to create, critique, and discuss print and nonprint texts.

- Use spoken, written, and visual language to accomplish a purpose (e.g., for learning, enjoyment, persuasion, and the exchange of information).

Objective

Students will identify different propaganda techniques used in media and then apply their knowledge by creating their own advertisement.

Materials

Propaganda Techniques reproducible
Product Summary reproducible
Print Ad Organizer reproducible
Commercial Ad Organizer reproducible
examples of print advertisements (and videotaped commercials)
old magazines and newspapers
scissors
poster board
art supplies

The power the media holds over consumers is tremendous. As students become more actively involved as consumers in the commercial marketplace, they need to become more aware of the influences used in print ads and commercials to make products more enticing to buyers. This activity will help students understand different propaganda techniques typically used in businesses and challenge them to use some of those same strategies to create their own advertisement campaign.

1. Gather examples of print advertisements (and if possible, some videotaped commercials) that employ the five main propaganda techniques: bandwagon, emotional plea, transfer, repetition, and testimonial. Also gather old magazines and newspapers for students to skim through and find propaganda to cut out.

2. Display and read aloud some of the print ads to the class (or show the videotaped commercials). Invite students to share their

thoughts about each sales pitch and tell which advertisements they think are the most convincing. Explain that there are five main strategies or propaganda techniques that advertisers use to lure customers to buy a particular product. List the five techniques on the board, and invite volunteers to share what they know about them. Then explain to students that they are going to learn more about those techniques and use them to promote and advertise their own products.

3. Divide the class into mixed-ability groups of five according to skill level and multiple intelligences. These are the base groups. Give each base group a copy of the **Propaganda Techniques reproducible (page 20)**, and have a student in each group cut apart the five cards and give one to each group member.

4. Have students with the same technique get together to form an expert group. Provide each expert group with some examples of their technique and a supply of newspapers and magazines. Have each group work together to read their definition card, review the examples, and cut from the newspapers and magazines at least ten more examples of their technique (two per person). The entire group must agree on all the advertisements selected for their examples.

5. Then have base groups reconvene and take turns sharing what they learned as experts. Remind students to check for understanding and make sure the entire group understands all five propaganda techniques. Write questions on the board for students to discuss with their group, such as:
   - *What kind of propaganda would use a celebrity to tell about a product?*
   - *What kind of propaganda would use a picture of a sad child?*
   - *What kind of propaganda would use a jingle played continuously in the background?*
   - *What kind of propaganda do you think would work better to convince young children? Teenagers? Young adults? Seniors?*

6. After students have had time to share and discuss their knowledge of propaganda techniques, introduce the next phase of the project: to invent and promote a product that appeals to middle school students. Explain that each group is responsible for inventing a product, making a model or poster of it, and developing an advertisement campaign that includes both a print advertisement and a video or theatrical commercial using at least one of the propaganda techniques.

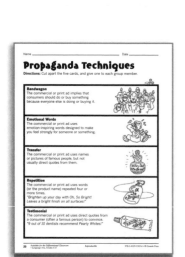

Propaganda Techniques Page 20

7. Tell groups to brainstorm ideas for their product and then decide together which product to make (and get your approval before making it). Give each group a copy of the **Product Summary**, **Print Ad Organizer**, and **Commercial Ad Organizer reproducibles (pages 21–23)** to help them plan and prepare their presentations.

▶

Product Summary Page 21

8. Allow several class sessions for students to complete this assignment. Suggest that they write a to-do list and assign responsibilities equally among group members. Remind them to cooperatively gather the supplies they need, design and create their product (a model or poster), develop the print advertisement, and create a commercial (presented live or on videotape). Encourage students to be persuasive, creative, dramatic, and appealing to their audience.

9. Set aside time for each group to present their product and ad campaign. Invite audience members to critique each presentation, evaluating the following categories: product idea, consumer appeal, creativity in product design and marketing, successful use of propaganda techniques, and overall presentation.

Name _____ Date _____

Propaganda Techniques

Directions: Cut apart the five cards, and give one to each group member.

Bandwagon
The commercial or print ad implies that consumers should do or buy something because everyone else is doing or buying it.

Emotional Words
The commercial or print ad uses emotion-inspiring words designed to make you feel strongly for someone or something.

Transfer
The commercial or print ad uses names or pictures of famous people, but not usually direct quotes from them.

Repetition
The commercial or print ad uses words (or the product name) repeated four or more times.
"Brighten up your day with Oh, So Bright! Leaves a bright finish on all surfaces!"

Testimonial
The commercial or print ad uses direct quotes from a consumer (often a famous person) to convince.
"9 out of 10 dentists recommend Pearly Whites!"

Product Summary

Directions: Complete this summary about your product.

Product Name: _____

Purpose of the Product: _____

_____

Description of the Product: _____

_____

_____

Reasons to Buy: _____

Where to Buy: _____

_____

Price: _____

Picture of the Product:

Print Ad Organizer

Directions: Use the organizer below to help you develop a print advertisement to sell your product.

Product Name: _____

Product Slogan: _____

_____

_____

Contents of Your Print Advertisement

_____

_____

_____

_____

Layout (Sketch) of Your Print Advertisement

Commercial Ad Organizer

Directions: Use the organizer below to help you develop a commercial advertisement to sell your product.

Product Name: _____

Product Jingle: _____

Goal of Your Commercial: _____

_____

_____

_____

Summary of Your Commercial: _____

_____

_____

Setting for Your Commercial: _____

_____

Actors Needed:

_____

_____

_____

_____

Props and Other Supplies Needed:

_____

_____

_____

_____

On another sheet of paper, write a script for your commercial. Include dialogue and stage directions. Make copies for all of your actors. Include a copy stapled to this cover sheet for your director. Be sure to rehearse your commercial before presenting it to an audience.

Word Wars

Strategy
Game

Standard

Apply a wide range of strategies to comprehend, interpret, evaluate, and appreciate texts. Draw on prior experience, interactions with other readers and writers, knowledge of word meaning and of other texts, word identification strategies, and understanding of textual features (e.g., sound-letter correspondence, sentence structure, context, graphics).

Objective

Students will learn new vocabulary by using cues and miscues in a game format.

Material

Word Wars Word Cards reproducible
cardstock, scissors, paper clips
markers and paper strips in three corresponding colors (e.g., red, blue, green)

Understanding key terminology used in nonfiction text and literary work is crucial for reading comprehension, but the process of learning new words can sometimes be tedious. This activity turns the task from tedious to exciting as students play a fun-filled variation of the interactive game *Balderdash*.

Word Wars Word Cards Page 26

1. In advance, photocopy the **Word Wars Word Cards reproducible (page 26)** onto cardstock. Use the cards to write 15 new vocabulary words and their correct definitions. Cut apart the word cards, and write a circled *C* next to each definition to keep track of correct answers during the game.

2. On the board, write and number the 15 vocabulary words for the class to preview. Explain to students that they will play a vocabulary version of the game *Balderdash* and try to figure out which definition is correct for each word.

Word: **Boycott**

Verb
To refuse to buy or
use a product or service
Ⓒ

Word: **Boycott**

Noun
A cot for boys

3. Divide the class into three mixed-ability teams—Team 1, Team 2, and Team 3—and give each team a copy of the Word Wars Word Cards reproducible. Tell teams to cut apart the cards, distribute them equally among teammates, and decide which vocabulary words from the board to assign to each person. On each card, students write the vocabulary word and a false but believable definition for that word.

4. Have teammates check each other's definitions and write their team number on the bottom their cards. Have them put their cards in the order listed on the board.

5. Collect the cards for each word, adding your definitions, and paperclip each set. On the board, create a tally chart with the titles *Choice 1, Choice 2, Choice 3, Choice 4*. Draw another chart with the titles *Team 1, Team 2, Team 3*, using a different color for each team. Distribute corresponding colors of paper strips to each team (one strip per student).

6. To play the game, read aloud a set of word cards and have students vote for the definition they think is correct. Read each set of cards twice, allowing students to first listen to all the definitions, and then hear each definition again, one at a time, to vote for their choice. Instruct students to hold up their colored paper to vote for their choice. Tally the votes by color, using the matching colored marker to draw the tallies for each choice. Then say the answer. Award points as follows:
   • Teams get one point for each teammate who votes for the correct definition.
   • Teams get one point for each opponent who votes for the incorrect definition.
   • The team with the most points at the end of the game wins!

Ideas for More Differentiation

Play the game in small groups according to readiness levels. For beginning mastery, have students draw pictures instead of write sentences to illustrate the meaning of each word. For approaching mastery, have students play the game as written. For high degree of mastery, have students use more advanced vocabulary words and/or include a sample sentence for each word.

Word Wars Word Cards

Directions: Cut out the cards, and distribute them to teammates. For each card, write a vocabulary word and an incorrect but believable definition for that word.

Word: _____	Word: _____	Word: _____
Word: _____	Word: _____	Word: _____
Word: _____	Word: _____	Word: _____
Word: _____	Word: _____	Word: _____
Word: _____	Word: _____	Word: _____

It's a Mystery

Standard

Read a wide range of literature from many periods in many genres to build an understanding of the many dimensions (e.g., philosophical, ethical, aesthetic) of human experience.

Strategies

Graphic organizer

Choice board

Objective

Students will read and analyze a mystery novel and then create a project about it.

Materials

Mystery Setting reproducible
Mystery Plot reproducible
Mystery Choice Board reproducible
Project Organizer reproducible
Book Review reproducible
collection of mystery novels at different reading levels
assorted supplies for student projects
index cards

With their intriguing characters and their gradually unfolding storylines, mysteries get even the most reluctant students excited about reading. They are great for teaching critical thinking skills and engaging higher-order levels of learning. In this activity, students put both their deductive reasoning and their creative thinking to work as they read, analyze, and interpret mysteries.

1. Collect a variety of mystery novels at different reading levels to meet students' needs. You may assign a specific novel to students or have them choose their own. Students may work by themselves or with a partner.

2. Give students a specific timeframe to finish their novel. Have them plan ahead, counting the number of chapters in their book and deciding how many chapters they must read per day or per week to meet that goal.

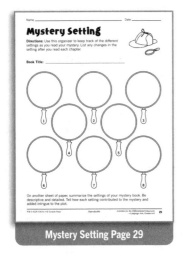

Mystery Setting Page 29

3. Provide time for students to read their novel in class as well as at home. Have them complete the **Mystery Setting** and **Mystery Plot reproducibles (pages 29–30)** as they read, filling in details after each chapter. (They will need more than one copy of the reproducibles if they have more than eight chapters.)

4. After students finish reading their novels, have them choose and complete a project from the **Mystery Choice Board reproducible (page 31)**. Then give them a copy of the **Project Organizer reproducible (page 32)** to plan and organize their project.

5. Provide time for students to share their finished projects with the class, or set up a display table of the projects for students to explore during free time.

Ideas for More Differentiation

Encourage students with a high degree of mastery to read more than one mystery novel and complete a **Book Review reproducible (page 33)** for each one. Place the finished reviews in a three-ring binder in alphabetical order by title. Encourage classmates to read the book reviews before deciding whether or not to read a particular book.

Book Review Page 33

Name _____   Date _____

Mystery Setting

Directions: Use this organizer to keep track of the different settings as you read your mystery. List any changes in the setting after you read each chapter.

Book Title: _____

1

2

3

4

5

6

7

8

On another sheet of paper, summarize the settings of your mystery book. Be descriptive and detailed. Tell how each setting contributed to the mystery and added intrigue to the plot.

Mystery Plot

Directions: Use this organizer to keep track of the plot as you read your mystery. Record events from each chapter.

Book Title: _____

On another sheet of paper, summarize the plot of your mystery in three parts—beginning, middle, and end. Write complete sentences. Tell how the mystery was solved.

Mystery Choice Board

Directions: Choose a project for your mystery novel. Work by yourself, with a partner, or with a group. List the supplies needed to complete the project.

Write and present a news interview of key witnesses and suspects.	Create a board game that includes clue cards and problem-solving challenges.	Work with classmates to act out a court trial in which the villain is being tried for his or her crime.
Design and write a front-page newspaper article about the mystery and how it was solved.	Create a movie poster and commercial for the book's movie release.	Pretend you are a spy, and create a dossier of one of the key characters.
Illustrate a comic book or cartoon strip of your mystery story.	Write at least five entries that could appear in the main character's diary.	Create a police flowchart, following the action of the mystery from introduction to solution.

Supplies Needed:

_____   _____

_____   _____

_____   _____

_____   _____

_____   _____

Name _____ Date _____

Project Organizer

Directions: Use the chart to help you plan and organize your project.

Project Goal	Parts of the Project

Step-by-Step Plan

↓

↓

↓

*Activities for the Differentiated Classroom
• Language Arts, Grades 6–8*   Reproducible   978-1-4129-5343-6 • © Corwin Press

Book Review

Directions: Imagine you are an important literary critic. Write a review of the book you just read, completing the information below. (Remember *not* to give away the ending or any surprises in the plot.) Color the stars to show your rating from 1 to 4. Color all four stars to show your highest recommendation.

Title of Book: _____

Author: _____

Number of Pages: _____

Synopsis: _____

_____

_____

_____

_____

_____

Rating:

What I Liked:

_____

_____

_____

_____

_____

What I Didn't Like:

_____

_____

_____

I would recommend this book to a friend (circle one):

YES   MAYBE   NO

Biography Blitz

Standards

- Read a wide range of literature from many periods in many genres to build an understanding of the many dimensions (e.g., philosophical, ethical, aesthetic) of human experience.

- Adjust the use of spoken, written, and visual language (e.g., conventions, style, vocabulary) to communicate effectively with a variety of audiences and for different purposes.

Objective

Students will role-play the main character of a biography and summarize that person's accomplishments.

Materials

Biography Overview reproducible
Biography Role-Play Guide reproducible

Biographies can provide role models for inspiring new attitudes and behaviors and can promote an appreciation of diversity. By dramatizing life stories, students become more thoughtful and reflective readers. In this activity, students identify and evaluate the critical parts of a biography and then role-play the main character in an oral presentation.

1. Gather a collection of biographies at different reading levels to meet students' varying needs, or provide a list from which students can choose. You may use online resources such as the InfoPlease®: Biographies at *www.infoplease.com/people.html* or Litopia: Profiles of Famous Americans at: *http://www.edwardsly. com/biography.html*. Include biographies of people from different countries and cultures.

2. Give students a copy of the **Biography Overview reproducible (page 36)**. Encourage them to use the outline to guide their reading. Suggest that they take notes as they read each chapter of their biography. Point out that they should gain an understanding of that person's life as well as get a sense of how that person thinks, acts, and feels.

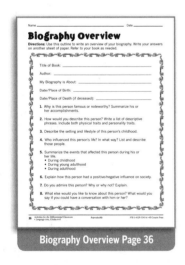

Biography Overview Page 36

3. After students finish reading their biographies and complete their Biography Overviews, announce that they are going to present a speech "in character" as the person featured in their biography. Instruct students to complete the **Biography Role-Play Guide reproducible (page 37)** to help them plan their performance. Check their speeches, and give them time to practice before performing for the class.

4. Have students role-play their oral presentation for the class, and invite classmates to ask each performer questions after his or her speech. Remind performers to stay in character and respond accordingly as that person. If possible, videotape students so they can review and self-assess their performances later.

Biography Role-Play Guide Page 37

Ideas for More Differentiation

Allow students who feel uncomfortable speaking in front of a group to refer to their Biography Role-Play Guide during their performance. Or, allow those students to videotape their performance at home and then play the tape in class.

Extend the Activity

• Host a meet-and-greet night for parents to see their children in action role-playing the characters. Have parents go from character to character as they would in a museum exhibit and listen to each presentation. Or students can take turns presenting themselves in character to the audience.

• Have students visit other classes and present themselves in character, or invite other classes to visit your room to see your "living museum of characters." Ask students to stand still in museum-like poses until a visitor touches them, at which time they "come alive" and talk about themselves in character (and then go back to their frozen position). Remind students to stay in character the whole time.

Biography Overview

Directions: Use this outline to write an overview of your biography. Write your answers on another sheet of paper. Refer to your book as needed.

Title of Book: _____

Author: _____

My Biography is About: _____

Date/Place of Birth: _____

Date/Place of Death (if deceased): _____

1. Why is this person famous or noteworthy? Summarize his or her accomplishments.

2. How would you describe this person? Write a list of descriptive phrases. Include both physical traits and personality traits.

3. Describe the setting and lifestyle of this person's childhood.

4. Who influenced this person's life? In what way? List and describe those people.

5. Summarize the events that affected this person during his or her life.
   • During childhood
   • During young adulthood
   • During adulthood

6. Explain how this person had a positive/negative influence on society.

7. Do you admire this person? Why or why not? Explain.

8. What else would you like to know about this person? What would you say if you could have a conversation with him or her?

Biography Role-Play Guide

Directions: Complete this guide to help you plan your performance. Remember to stay in character when you present yourself to the audience.

Who are you portraying? _____

What costume will you wear? _____

How will you present yourself? What will be your overall demeanor (mannerism, body language, facial expression, dialect) to help you portray your character?

_____

_____

What will you say to your audience? Write your monologue below. Include your (character's) name, where you lived, when you lived, why you're famous, and any interesting details about your life. Refer to your Biography Overview.

_____
_____
_____
_____
_____
_____
_____
_____
_____
_____

Black and White Puzzler

Strategies

Jigsaw

Graphic organizer

Standards

- Participate as knowledgeable, reflective, creative, and critical members of a variety of literacy communities.

- Apply a wide range of strategies to comprehend, interpret, evaluate, and appreciate texts. Draw on prior experience, interactions with other readers and writers, knowledge of word meaning and of other texts, word identification strategies, and understanding of textual features (e.g., sound-letter correspondence, sentence structure, context, graphics).

Objective

Students will analyze and discuss the interwoven plots of four different storylines in the picture book *Black and White*.

Materials

Black and White Story Map reproducible
Black and White Summary reproducible
several copies of the book *Black and White* by David Macaulay
large self-stick notes

Picture books can provide an opportunity for readers of all ages to explore meaningful topics, analyze a writer's craft, and appreciate artistic interpretation. In the picture book *Black and White*, readers are introduced to four seemingly separate stories that interweave throughout the book. By analyzing the twists and turns, students explore multiple meanings in both text and illustrations.

1. Gather several copies of the picture book *Black and White* by David Macaulay, at least one copy for each group of students. Use large self-stick notes to cover unassigned sections of each book before distributing them to the class, as follows:

   Group 1: Read only the upper left corner of each page.

   Group 2: Read only the upper right corner of each page.

   Group 3: Read only the lower left corner of each page.

   Group 4: Read only the lower right corner of each page.

   Group 5: Read all four corners of each page (the entire book).

2. Discuss with students the general format and purpose of picture books. They will read and analyze a rather unusual picture book.

3. Divide the class into five mixed-ability groups, and assign sections of the book to each group as directed in Step 1. (Assign more advanced readers to Group 5.) Instruct students not to remove any of the self-stick notes in their book.

4. Give each group a copy of the **Black and White Story Map reproducible (page 40)**. Have groups work together to finish the map after reading their section of the book. (Some areas of the story map may be left blank depending on the section assigned.)

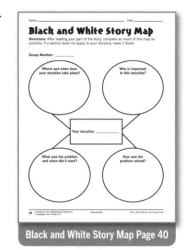

Black and White Story Map Page 40

5. Regroup all students, using one student from each original group to form a new group of five. Each new group should have one student from each original group.

6. Have students take turns sharing their story maps. Have them analyze and compare how the maps relate to each other (how each "corner story" map relates to the entire story map). Have students discuss how all four storylines interact throughout the book. Ask each group to complete a **Black and White Summary reproducible (page 41)** to record their findings and conclusions.

Black and White Summary Page 41

7. Invite each group to share what they discovered with the rest of the class, referring to their summary sheets. Have students share their thoughts and feelings about the book, using the following prompts to guide the discussion:
   - *How does Macaulay use illustrations to manage the time sequence in the book?*
   - *Why do you think Macaulay chose to use other colors on the book's cover, not just black and white as suggested by the title?*
   - *When we think of a picture book, we usually think of the illustrations as complementing the story. Is that true for this book? What are some examples where the illustrations clarify the story? contradict the story?*

Extend the Activity
Udder chaos is an example of a pun used in this book. Remind students that a *pun* is a play on words. Ask students to list other puns used in the book. Then invite them to write and illustrate their own puns. Display their work on a bulletin board, or bind the pages to make a class book.

Black and White Story Map

Directions: After reading your part of the story, complete as much of this map as possible. If a section does not apply to your storyline, leave it blank.

Group Number: _____

Where and when does
your storyline take place?

Who is important
to this storyline?

Your storyline: _____

What was the problem
and when did it start?

How was the
problem solved?

 *Activities for the Differentiated Classroom
• Language Arts, Grades 6–8*   *Reproducible*   978-1-4129-5343-6 • © Corwin Press

Black and White Summary

Directions: Record details about each storyline. Then use this chart to compare the storylines. Then draw an X in the corresponding box if that storyline includes the detail.

Details	Story 1	Story 2	Story 3	Story 3

Discuss and Write

• How does each single storyline tie in with the main story?

• How do all the storylines work together to allow the plot to progress?

• What relationships can be found among the lines, words, and illustrations?

_____

_____

_____

A Book a Day

Strategies

Cooperative group learning

Journaling

Presentation

Standards

- Read a wide range of print and nonprint texts to build an understanding of texts, of self, and of the cultures of the United States and the world; to acquire new information; to respond to the needs and demands of society and the workplace; and for personal fulfillment (including fiction and nonfiction, classic, and contemporary works).

- Use spoken, written, and visual language to accomplish a purpose (e.g., for learning, enjoyment, persuasion, and the exchange of information).

Objective

Students will work cooperatively to read and summarize a novel in one day.

Materials

A Book a Day Summary Sheet reproducible

class set of a novel

journals

poster board

art supplies

As the curriculum gets more and more crowded, there is often less time for students to enjoy the great many books available to them. This activity, which can be repeated throughout the year, provides students with the opportunity to "read" a lengthy book that they might not otherwise have time to read.

1. Gather enough copies of the same novel for the entire class. List the chapters on the board, and separate them into sections—one or two chapters per section.

2. Divide the class into mixed-ability groups, the same number of groups as there are sections of the book, and assign a different section to each group. Have students take turns reading aloud each paragraph or page of their section as the rest of the group follows along.

3. Monitor the class as they work. Suggest that students stop reading after each page and jot down notes in their journal about what they just read. Tell them to summarize the setting, the characters, and the plot. Suggest that they write an *S* by notes about the setting, a *C* by notes about the characters, and a *P* by notes about the plot.

4. After they finish reading their sections of the book, give each group poster board and a copy of the **A Book a Day Summary Sheet reproducible (page 44)**. Tell groups to follow the directions to make a poster about their section of the book. Encourage students to be creative, draw pictures, invent symbols, and write descriptive words to summarize the people, places, and events in the story.

5. Ask each group to present their section of the book in consecutive order, giving the class the opportunity to hear the book in its entirety, from beginning to end. Invite students to predict what will happen next in the story, before each group shares their section. Make a plot flowchart on the board, adding information after each presentation. After all groups have shared their part of the story, review the flowchart with students and summarize the book's entire plot.

6. Display the posters on a bulletin board, or bind them together to create a "big book" of the novel for the whole class to enjoy.

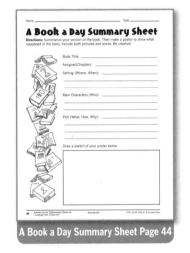

A Book a Day Summary Sheet Page 44

Ideas for More Differentiation

For ELL students and students approaching mastery, you might provide a copy of the book on audiotape so they can listen while they read.

Extend the Activity

Have small groups of students work together to read more novels cooperatively with each group taking responsibility for reading a certain part of the book and then summarizing it for the rest of the class.

A Book a Day Summary Sheet

Directions: Summarize your section of the book. Then make a poster to show what happened in the story. Include both pictures and words. Be creative!

Book Title: _____

Assigned Chapters: _____

Setting (Where, When): _____

_____

_____

Main Characters (Who): _____

_____

_____

Plot (What, How, Why): _____

_____

_____

_____

Draw a sketch of your poster below.

978-1-4129-5343-6 • © Corwin Press

CHAPTER 2

Writing

Censor the Censor!

Strategies

Focus activity

Journaling

Standard

Employ a wide range of strategies while writing, and use different writing process elements appropriately to communicate with different audiences for a variety of purposes.

Objective

Students will use visual strategies to overcome writer's block.

Materials

drawing paper
colored pencils or markers
thick red markers

Getting ideas down on paper can sometimes be the toughest task for young writers. In this simple focus activity, students are able to overcome their writer's block and feel free jotting down anything that comes to mind!

1. Explain to students that sometimes a censor can get in the way of a person's ability to write. (If your students are unfamiliar with the word *censor,* explain that a censor is a critic or faultfinder whose purpose is to suppress or prohibit.) This censor could be someone students are afraid of disappointing, or their own belief that they are not good writers.

2. Tell students that they will symbolically silence their own censor once and for all. Distribute drawing paper, and instruct students to draw whatever monster they envision as their censor. Hideous, comical, realistic, fantastical—whatever they imagine.

3. Once their drawings are finished, distribute thick red markers and instruct students to draw a thick red circle around their censor, with a line drawn diagonally across the center. They have just silenced their censor forever!

4. Set a timer for 10 minutes, and tell students to brainstorm in writing anything that comes to mind when they think of the word *censor.* Tell them that the goal is to keep writing until you tell

them to stop. If they run out of things to write before then, they can just write *I don't know what to write,* over and over again until they think of something else. Suggest that they refer to their picture to spark ideas.

5. After the exercise, invite volunteers to share their feelings about the experience. Point out that even the most famous writers experience writer's block and go through similar exercises to open up their mind and get the words to flow.

6. Invite volunteers to share their pictures and read aloud what they wrote. Display the pictures around the classroom, or have students store their pictures in their writing folders. Encourage students to look at their picture whenever they experience writer's block.

Ideas for More Differentiation

Review students' writing samples to gain a better understanding of their thoughts and feelings about writing. Meet with them individually to address their needs.

Extend the Activity

You can use a similar writing strategy throughout the year to promote fluency of thinking and give students the opportunity to let their thoughts flow freely on paper. Provide students with a specific writing prompt, or just have them write anything that comes to mind for the entire time period. You might also have them keep a specific journal or notebook for recording their thoughts.

Writing Cube

Standard
Employ a wide range of strategies while writing, and use different writing process elements appropriately to communicate with different audiences for a variety of purposes.

Strategy
Cubing

Objective
Students will research and write about a topic from six different perspectives.

Materials
Writing Cube reproducible
index cards
colored paper
scissors
paper bag
tape

This cubing activity gives students the opportunity to consider a topic from six different points of view, developing a multidimensional understanding rather than a single perspective. The cubes may be created with tasks or commands that are appropriate for different ability levels, or they may be created with tasks in a particular area of the multiple intelligences, such as verbal/linguistic, bodily/kinesthetic, or intrapersonal.

1. On index cards, write different topics you'd like students to review and explore in their writing. Focus on books or topics the class is currently reading or studying.

2. Use the **Writing Cube reproducible (page 49)** to make several task cubes that vary in ability levels or multiple intelligences. (You might recruit some students to help you make the cubes.) You can distinguish the cube levels by color, writing the prompts on different colored paper. Or, write numbers *1–6* on the sides of the cubes and make topic cards at various levels of complexity to accompany them (also numbered *1–6*). Use a variety of verbs and commands for each side of the cubes. For example: *Name it; Describe it; Compare and contrast it with something else; Draw a cartoon or comic strip; Associate it with something else; Summarize it.*

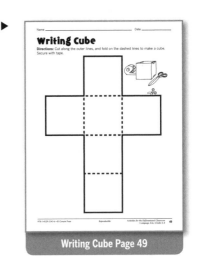

Writing Cube Page 49

3. Divide the class into groups of six students. Group students according to their readiness levels, and distribute the cubes accordingly.

4. Have groups choose a topic card from the bag. Instruct them to use the prompts on the cube to prepare a written response to their topic. Each group member rolls the cube to find out his or her assignment. Or, allow students to choose a topic that fits their ability level or learning style.

5. Allow several days for groups to complete the assignment. Invite them to take turns presenting their results to the class.

Ideas for More Differentiation

Assign beginning mastery students a vocabulary word instead of a topic card. Give them a Writing Cube reproducible with the following prompts written on the sides: *Word; Definition; Part of Speech; Synonyms; Anonyms; Sample Sentences.* Have them complete the information about their vocabulary word on the actual cube and then cut out and tape the cube together.

Writing Cube

Directions: Cut along the outer lines, and fold on the dashed lines to make a cube. Secure with tape.

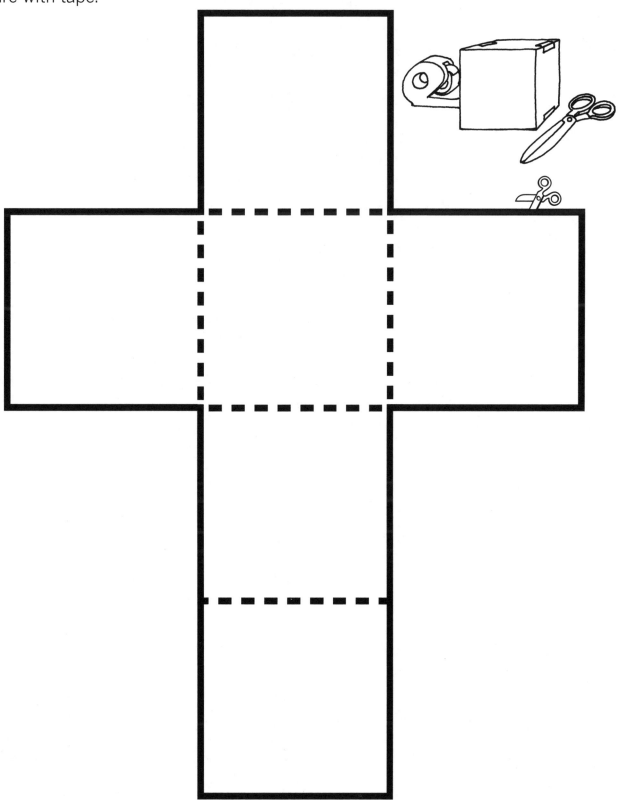

Tree Down in the Park

Strategies

Role play

Reflection after learning

Standards

- Use spoken, written, and visual language to accomplish a purpose (e.g., for learning, enjoyment, persuasion, and the exchange of information).

- Develop an understanding of and respect for diversity in language use, patterns, and dialects across cultures, ethnic groups, geographic regions, and social roles.

Objective

Students will role-play and write about an unexpected event from the point of view of a chosen character and then write a newspaper report based on these different perspectives.

Materials

writing paper or journals
video recorder (optional)

In this activity, students step out of their own character and into the role of another, reacting to a situation from that person's point of view. Through role-playing and reflective writing, students learn an important lesson about how to appreciate different perspectives and walk a mile in another person's shoes.

1. Brainstorm with students a list of different people and activities that might be seen at a park, and write those ideas on the board. For example: *a family having a picnic, little leaguers playing baseball, a parent and child on the playground, seniors playing checkers, a father and son flying a kite, an elderly woman on a bench feeding the birds.*

2. Have each student choose one of those characters and imagine themselves in the park. Prompt them to consider what they would be thinking and doing as that character. Give them a few minutes to quietly imagine themselves in that role.

3. Have students move their desks to the perimeter of the classroom and stand in the center of the room. Tell them to imagine that they are now at a park. Have them role-play their characters, interacting with each other and the park setting. Suggest that they role-play activities and use dialects and language patterns appropriate for their character's age, culture, and social role.

4. Give the class several minutes to get fully into character. Once you are sure students are fully engaged in their roles and not watching you, suddenly slam a book or drop a heavy object on the floor. After students react to the loud noise, announce that a large, old oak tree in the park has just toppled over and crashed down in the parking lot. Nobody has been hurt, but a lot of cars have been damaged.

5. Tell students to return to their desks and write about what just happened at the park, including what they saw and heard and their thoughts, feelings, and reactions from the point of view of their characters. Encourage them to close their eyes and imagine the event before they start writing about it.

6. Divide the class into small groups, each with different characters. Have them read and discuss what they wrote about the event. Encourage them to analyze and compare the different responses and reactions of the characters.

7. Continue the writing activity by having each group work together to write a newspaper article about the event. They can compile information from what they already wrote or choose a student to conduct an interview with each character. Have one or two group members take notes on the interviews.

8. When the interviews are done, have groups compile the notes into a newspaper article. Remind students that their articles should encompass different points of view and answer the questions *who, what, when, where, why,* and *how.*

9. Conclude the activity by having each group read aloud their newspaper article. Invite students to share their thoughts and observations—how they viewed their own character, how they viewed other characters, and whether or not they saw a character the same way as someone else. (For example, if two students were role-playing a parent at the park with children, did they both have the same reaction to the crash, or did their own prejudices cause them to see the same event in different ways?)

10. Encourage students to speculate on how this activity relates to real-life people and events outside of school and how they might use what they've learned from it.

Ideas for More Differentiation

Before students write independently, give them a few minutes to discuss their ideas with a partner. You might also suggest that they brainstorm words and phrases describing their character's thoughts and feelings before they start writing their narrative. Provide writing prompts, such as: *What were you thinking and doing just before you heard the crash? What was your reaction to the noise? What was your first thought and reaction after the noise?*

Extend the Activity

Have a student in each group act as a reporter on the scene, interviewing the others for the nightly news. If possible, videotape these interviews and show them to the class so students can observe and self-assess their own performance.

Metaphor Match

Standard
Apply knowledge of language structure, language conventions (e.g., spelling and punctuation), media techniques, figurative language, and genre to create, critique, and discuss print and nonprint texts.

Objective
Students will write and illustrate metaphors about dissimilar objects.

Materials
index cards
paper bag

Strategy
Metaphor

Figurative language is a tool authors use to help readers creatively visualize what is happening in a story or poem. In this activity, students explore figurative language through the use of metaphors, writing creative sentences to compare dissimilar objects.

1. Before starting this activity, make a set of 40 or more word cards using the names of animals, common objects, items found in nature, and objects mentioned in recent class novels or lessons. Place the cards in a paper bag for students to choose at random during the activity.

2. Review figurative language with students, and explain that they will be working with metaphors. Discuss the differences between similes and metaphors.
   - *A simile* usually compares two dissimilar objects using the words *like* or *as*.
   - *A metaphor* is a direct comparison that does not use the words *like* or *as* and may state that one thing is actually something else.

3. Write the following examples on the board, and have students identify which are metaphors and which are similes:
   - *She runs like the wind.* (simile)
   - *He's as strong as an ox.* (simile)
   - *My little brother is a monster.* (metaphor)
   - *You have a heart of gold.* (metaphor)
   - *I have a mountain of work.* (metaphor)
   - *We're like two peas in a pod.* (simile)

4. Invite two volunteers to each pick a word card from the bag, and write the words on the board. Ask the class to brainstorm metaphors comparing the two objects. Write their suggestions on the board. Instruct them to use only pronouns and names of literary characters (no names of real people).

5. Then have each student or pair of students take two cards from the bag and write metaphors about the words on their own. Suggest that they first brainstorm ways the objects are alike before they write their metaphors. Encourage students to draw illustrations of their metaphors after they write them.

6. Provide time for students to share their metaphors with the class. Ask the class to add ideas to each metaphor.

Ideas for More Differentiation

Encourage students with a high degree of mastery to write and illustrate a short dialogue or story that includes creative metaphors. For beginning mastery students, write the following metaphors on index cards. Invite them to choose a card and illustrate the metaphor.

- *Breaking news*
- *Bursting with flavor*
- *Stubborn stains*
- *Caged emotions*
- *A flood of emotions*
- *A storm of controversy*
- *A window of opportunity*
- *She melted at the sight of him.*
- *He's dying to meet her.*
- *That guy is rock solid.*

Picture Poems

Standards

- Employ a wide range of strategies while writing, and use different writing process elements appropriately to communicate with different audiences for a variety of purposes.

- Apply knowledge of language structure, language conventions (e.g., spelling and punctuation), media techniques, figurative language, and genre to create, critique, and discuss print and nonprint texts.

Objective

Students will write poetry about photographs they have taken outdoors.

Materials

Picture Poems reproducible
digital or disposable cameras
manila envelopes
colorful art paper
cardstock
glue

In this activity, the phrase *a picture is worth a thousand words* is put into play as students use poetic verse and imagery to interpret and describe photographs of their environment.

1. Do this activity on a day when the weather is sunny and clear. Gather several disposable or digital cameras, one for each group of students. Write a different number on each camera (and later use those same numbers on the developer's envelopes to keep track of the pictures from each camera).

2. Divide the class into mixed-ability groups, and give each group a camera. Explain that they will be walking around campus taking pictures and writing notes of images that inspire them. Before they go outdoors, have each group write their camera number in a notebook.

3. Have students walk around campus in their groups, taking turns using the cameras. Instruct them to each take three to five pictures of different things that capture their attention or spark their imagination. Tell students to write brief notes after taking each picture so they'll

recognize their photos later on. Encourage them to also record any textures, sounds, and aromas they observe.

4. Have the pictures developed, and put each set of photographs in different envelopes, numbering them to correspond with the cameras. Distribute the envelopes to students.

◀ **Picture Poems Page 57**

5. Use an overhead transparency of the **Picture Poems reproducible (page 57)** and a student's photograph to demonstrate how to write impressions about the image. Explain that you will use those ideas to write a poem. Ask students to help you list different types of poems on the board, such as *acrostic, cinquain, haiku, limerick,* and *rhyming poems (couplets, triplets, quatrains)*. Work together to write several different poems about the picture.

6. Invite students to write their own poems about their photographs. They may write a different poem for each picture or a long narrative poem about all of them combined. Tell students to first complete the Picture Poems reproducible about their photographs.

7. Have partners proofread each other's poems before writing their final drafts. Instruct students to type their final versions or use artistic handwriting on colorful art paper. Finally, have them glue their final versions onto cardstock along with the photographs.

8. Invite volunteers to show their photos and read their poems aloud. Display all of the poems on a bulletin board, or bind the pages together to make a class book.

Ideas for More Differentiation

Invite your musical/rhythmic students to write raps or ballads about their photographs and perform them for the class. You could also host an open mic session of poetry reading, transforming your room into a coffee shop!

Picture Poems

Directions: Complete this organizer to help you write your poem.

Title of your photograph.

Describe your photograph.

Explain how it makes you feel (your emotions).

Use similes and metaphors to compare it to other things.

Discuss why it is important.

Story Sparklers

Strategies

Cooperative group learning

Problem-based learning

Graphic organizer

Standard

Employ a wide range of strategies while writing, and use different writing process elements appropriately to communicate with different audiences for a variety of purposes.

Objective

Students will work in cooperative groups to write a creative story about mismatched characters in an unusual setting with a specific problem to solve.

Materials

Story Web reproducible
Story Picture Cards reproducible
index cards
tape

This activity will help your students feel more comfortable speaking in front of their peers and foster cooperative skills as they work together to create imaginative stories. They will especially enjoy the element of surprise as they randomly choose characters, settings, and story conflicts.

1. Review with students the main elements that make up a story: characters, setting, problem, sequence of events, and solution.

2. Write *characters, setting,* and *problem* on the board, and tape index cards below the words. Ask students to brainstorm suggestions for each topic as you write their ideas on the cards. They may suggest people, places, and problems from novels, movies, and television shows as well as from real life. For example: *Harry Potter, Queen Elizabeth, Mickey Mouse, Grandpa Joe; dark cavern, ghost town, country road, Mount Everest; broken foot, car without gasoline, unexpected storm, unwelcome visitor.* Place the cards in three separate stacks facedown.

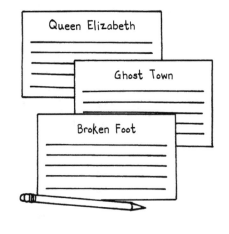

3. Divide the class into mixed-ability groups of four, and have each group choose one card from each pile to form a set of story starters. (If there are enough cards, students may choose two character cards.) Tell groups to work together to write a creative story about their cards. Their story should have a clear beginning, middle, and end and should include many descriptive details.

4. Before they start writing, have each group complete a **Story Web reproducible (page 60)** to help them organize and discuss their ideas. Point out that they need to decide on a sequence of events and a solution to the problem.

5. Check students' Story Webs to make sure their ideas are complete before they begin writing their stories. You might also check their rough drafts before they write (or type) their final versions.

6. Encourage group members to take on different roles according to their preferred learning styles. For example, the verbal/linguistic learners can write the group's ideas and suggestions; bodily/kinesthetic learners can role-play suggestions for dialogue or action; logical/mathematical learners can type the final draft on a computer; visual/spatial learners can draw pictures to go with the story.

7. Invite each group to read their story aloud to the class. Group members can take turns reading each part of their story or choose one person to read it all.

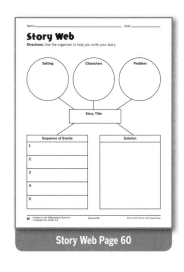

Story Web Page 60

Ideas for More Differentiation

• Encourage students with a high degree of mastery to write stories that include multiple storylines, such as a mystery with several characters and conflicts.

• Have beginning mastery students write a story about a set of picture cards instead of word cards. Give them a set of **Story Picture Cards (page 61)** or cutouts from magazines and newspapers. Encourage English Language Learners to write a story in their native language and then partner with fluent bilingual students to translate their their story into English.

Story Picture Cards Page 61

Name _____ Date _____

Story Web

Directions: Use the organizer to help you write your story.

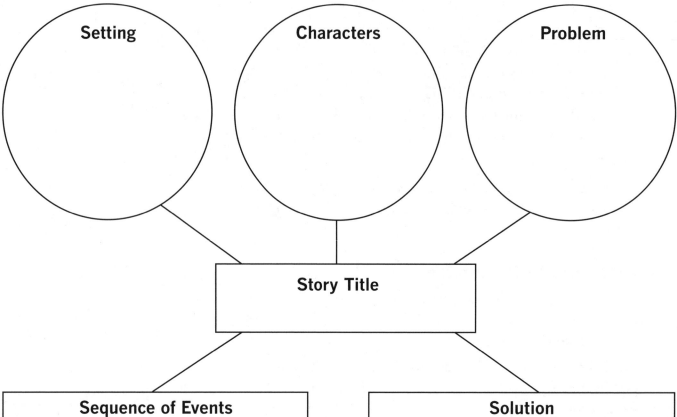

Setting

Characters

Problem

Story Title

Sequence of Events
1.
2.
3.
4.
5.

Solution

 Activities for the Differentiated Classroom • Language Arts, Grades 6–8   Reproducible   978-1-4129-5343-6 • © Corwin Press

Story Picture Cards

Tricky Tongue Twisters

Strategy
Rhymes

Standards

- Apply knowledge of language structure, language conventions (e.g., spelling and punctuation), media techniques, figurative language, and genre to create, critique, and discuss print and nonprint texts.

- Develop an understanding of and respect for diversity in language use, patterns, and dialects across cultures, ethnic groups, geographic regions, and social roles.

Objective

Students will use their knowledge of alliteration to write tongue twisters.

Materials

Tricky Tongue Twisters reproducible
dictionaries
drawing paper
colored pencils or markers

In this activity, students apply their knowledge of word structure and different parts of speech to create challenging and humorous language patterns in the form of tongue twisters.

1. Explain to students that a *tongue twister* is a sequence of words that is difficult to articulate quickly and that often contains alliteration (words that begin with the same letter). Share some examples, and have students repeat them as fast as they can:
   - *A noisy noise annoys an oyster.*
   - *We shall surely see the sunshine soon.*
   - *Brad's big black bath brush broke.*

2. Use the following model to demonstrate how to form a tongue twister:
   - Use at least one noun. (*Sally, seagulls, soup*)
   - Use at least one verb. (*saw, slurp*)
   - Use several adjectives. (*six, silly, slimy*)
   - Use at least one adverb. (*sloppily*)
   - Use at least one prepositional phrase. (*by the seashore*)

3. Invite students to use some or all of the words to say different tongue twisters. For example:

- *Sally saw six silly seagulls slurp slimy soup sloppily by the seashore.*
- *Six slimy seagulls saw silly Sally slurp soup sloppily by the seashore.*
- *Six silly seagulls sloppily slurp slimy soup.*

4. Distribute the **Tricky Tongue Twisters reproducible (page 64)**, and ask students to write their own challenging tongue twisters using other words. Suggest that they brainstorm several words and try different combinations to write a few creative tongue twisters. Encourage them to look up and use new words from a dictionary.

5. Have students type their tongue twisters and draw pictures to accompany them. Students can share their tongue twisters in small groups.

6. Compile the pages together to make a class book. You might also make photocopies of the book so each student can have his or her own copy.

7. Invite students to read aloud some of their tongue twisters for classmates to repeat. Or, have a tongue-twisting contest, challenging students to say a specific tongue twister correctly in the shortest amount of time.

Tricky Tongue Twisters Page 64

Ideas for More Differentiation

Invite students to collect and share other tongue twisters, including those written in other languages. Here are some possible resources:

- *International Collection of Tongue Twisters:* http://www.uebersetzung.at/twister/en.htm

- *Tongue Twister Database:* www.geocities.com/Athens/8136/tonguetwisters.html

- *Tongue Twisters in Spanish:* www.ccs.neu.edu/home/gene/tongue-twisters.html

- *Ridiculous Tongue Twisters* by Chris Tait and Buck Jones

- *World's Toughest Tongue Twisters* by Joseph Rosenbloom and Dennis Kendrick

Tricky Tongue Twisters

Directions: Write a list of words in the balloons. Then use some or all of those words to write different tongue twisters on the lines below.

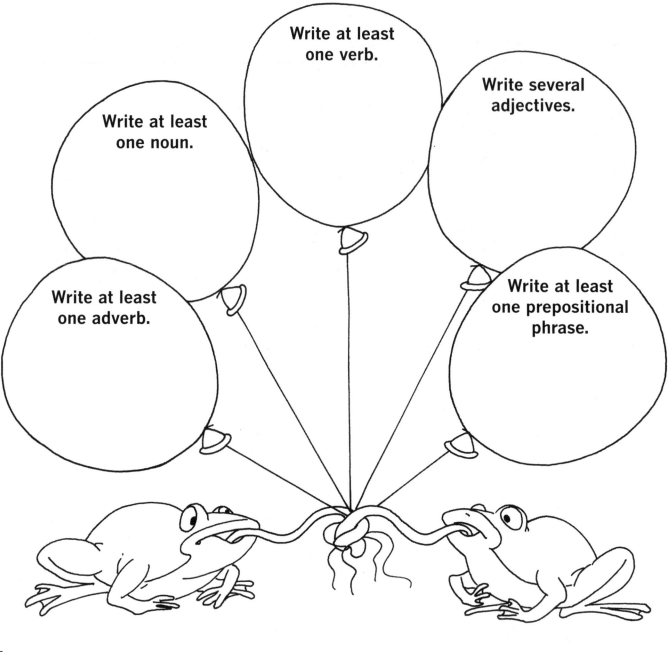

1. _____

2. _____

3. _____

4. _____

Reproducible   978-1-4129-5343-6 • © Corwin Press

Hand in Hand

Standard

Use spoken, written, and visual language to accomplish a purpose (e.g., for learning, enjoyment, persuasion, and the exchange of information).

Objective

Students will write their impressions of a handshake and reflect on other forms of nonverbal communication.

Materials

drawing paper
scissors
tape

A simple handshake is a powerful form of nonverbal communication. In this activity, students explore this type of silent communication and use it as a springboard for descriptive and reflective writing.

1. Invite students to list situations in which they might receive a handshake, such as at social gatherings, business meetings, and interviews. Explain that a simple handshake can convey a variety of meanings. You will be walking through the classroom shaking their hands. Ask them to pay close attention to the handshake and how it makes them feel because they will be writing about it.

2. Shake each student's hand a different way. Give some students a firm grip; others, a limp handshake. You can link pinkies and swing your hand playfully or clasp a student's wrist.

3. After you shake everyone's hand, give each student a sheet of drawing paper. Instruct students to trace their hand on the paper and write about their handshake in the outline. Tell them to write as descriptively as possible so that someone reading it could demonstrate the handshake accurately. Tell them to write about both the physical handshake and the way it made them feel.

4. Invite students to read their descriptions aloud and share their thoughts about the activity. Have them cut out their paper hands and tape them together to make a border around the classroom.

Extend the Activity

Have students demonstrate and write about other forms of nonverbal communication, such as eye contact and body stance. Discuss how these cues might be interpreted differently in other cultures.

CHAPTER 3

Language Conventions

Where's My Word Partner?

Standards

- Apply knowledge of language structure, language conventions (e.g., spelling and punctuation), media techniques, figurative language, and genre to create, critique, and discuss print and nonprint texts.

- Apply a wide range of strategies to comprehend, interpret, evaluate, and appreciate texts. Draw on prior experience, interactions with other readers and writers, knowledge of word meaning and of other texts, word identification strategies, and understanding of textual features (e.g., sound-letter correspondence, sentence structure, context, graphics).

Objective

Students will form, define, and use compound words in writing.

Materials

Compound Words List reproducible
index cards
vocabulary notebooks (or writing paper)
dictionaries

Learning to put together words appropriately to form compound words is often overlooked in the middle grades, yet it is a valuable tool for students' developing higher-level language skills. This activity gives students the opportunity to practice forming compound words.

Compound Words List Page 68

◄

1. Use the **Compound Words List reproducible (page 68)** to make two sets of word cards—one set with the first half of each compound word and the other set with the second half of each compound word. Prepare enough index cards for each student to have one card. (If there is an uneven number, you will play too.)

2. Mix up all the cards, and have each student choose one. Remind students that a *compound word* is formed when two words are joined to make a new word (usually with a different meaning).

Then tell students to find their word partner and make a compound word. (Partners should sit down when they find each other.)

3. Once everyone has found their partner, have each pair read their compound word to the class, and list the words on the board.

4. Then have the class use dictionaries or computer resources to find the definitions of all the compound words listed on the board. Have them write each definition and a sample sentence in their vocabulary notebooks.

5. Invite students to add the words and definitions in alphabetical order to the classroom Word Wall.

6. Challenge students to use the new words in classroom conversations and writing assignments. You might even keep a tally of the number of times students use the compound words that day or that week.

Ideas for More Differentiation

- To help beginning mastery students find their partner, provide them a compound-word list at the beginning of the activity.

- Invite students to draw visual interpretations of their compound words. For example, they could draw a raindrop wrapped in a bow for the word *rainbow*.

- Encourage visual/spatial and verbal/ linguistic learners to make crossword puzzles and word games using the compound words.

Extend the Activity

Use this activity throughout the year to mix things up, get students moving, or to help them learn new vocabulary. You might also use this activity (or a similar one involving other word pairs) as a creative way to pair up students for a project.

Compound Words List

airport	hamburger	spokesperson
alongside	headquarters	subway
anybody	housekeeper	homemade
babysitter	inside	household
backbone	keyboard	sunflower
backpack	lifeguard	supermarket
backstage	lifelong	supernatural
backward	lifetime	supersonic
baseball	limestone	superstructure
because	lukewarm	themselves
become	meantime	therefore
blacksmith	moonlight	throwback
bookcase	moreover	thunderstorm
butterfly	nobody	today
bypass	nowhere	toothpick
cannot	pacemaker	touchdown
crosswalk	passport	township
doorknob	peppermint	underage
earthquake	pickup	undercharge
elsewhere	popcorn	underground
everything	rainbow	uplift
eyeball	railroad	upside
firefly	rattlesnake	upstream
fireworks	sandstone	waterfall
footprint	scapegoat	weatherman
forefinger	something	whatever
forehead	sometimes	widespread
forklift	southwest	windmill
grandmother	spearmint	without

978-1-4129-5343-6 • © Corwin Press

A Prepositional Perspective

Standards

- Use spoken, written, and visual language to accomplish a purpose (e.g., for learning, enjoyment, persuasion, and the exchange of information).

- Apply knowledge of language structure, language conventions (e.g., spelling and punctuation), media techniques, figurative language, and genre to create, critique, and discuss print and nonprint texts.

Strategies

Role play

Multiple intelligences

Objective

Students will use prepositional phrases to interact with and describe objects in their environment.

In this activity, students demonstrate their understanding of prepositional phrases by describing and drawing floor plans—an approach that will especially appeal to your bodily/kinesthetic and visual/spatial learners.

1. Remind students that *prepositions* are often positional words that describe the location or spatial arrangement of objects. Tell them that you will be saying different prepositional phrases for them to demonstrate in the classroom.

2. Say prepositional phrases such as *under your desk, on the floor,* or *beside your chair.* Occasionally say a phrase without the preposition, asking students to anticipate it. For example: *your desk—under your desk, next to your desk, around your desk.*

3. Once students have a firm understanding of prepositions and prepositional phrases, tell them to write a paragraph describing the spatial arrangement of the furniture and other objects in their bedroom. They must include the following phrases, along with any others they choose: *in the corner, next to the bed, on top of the dresser, in the middle of the room, under the window.*

4. Have student pairs exchange papers and try to draw their partner's bedroom floor plan by following the written directions.

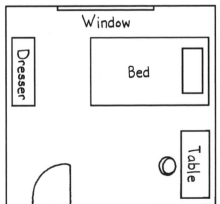

Ideas for More Differentiation

- For beginning mastery students, write a list of phrases, only some of them prepositional phrases. Have students identify which ones are prepositional phrases.

Prepositional Treasure Hunt

Strategies

Problem-based learning

Open-ended project

Standard

Use spoken, written, and visual language to accomplish a purpose (e.g., for learning, enjoyment, persuasion, and the exchange of information).

Objective

Students will apply their understanding of prepositional phrases to write and interpret directions for a treasure hunt.

Materials

Preposition Treasure Hunt reproducible
items to hide for a treasure hunt
drawing paper
colored pencils or markers

Preposition Treasure Hunt Page 71

Students will love this rewarding activity of creating and using treasure maps. It provides them with the opportunity to use both their knowledge of prepositional phrases and their keen detective skills!

1. Divide the class into mixed-ability groups of two or three, and give each group a copy of the **Preposition Treasure Hunt reproducible (page 71)** and a small treasure (any small object that can be hidden on campus) to hide.

2. Tell each group to hide their treasure somewhere on campus and then write directions (or clues) and draw a map to lead others to it. Instruct students to use at least ten prepositions from the reproducible in their clues. Clues must be complete and clearly written.

3. Once they have hidden their treasure and completed their clues and map, have each group trade with another group and try to find each other's hidden treasure.

Ideas for More Differentiation

For beginning mastery students, you might choose to provide partially written directions for them to complete. Tell them to fill in the appropriate prepositions and directional words (e.g., *right, left, up, down, north, south*) on their treasure map.

Name _____   Date _____

Preposition Treasure Hunt

Directions: Use at least ten of these prepositions in the clues leading to your hidden treasure.

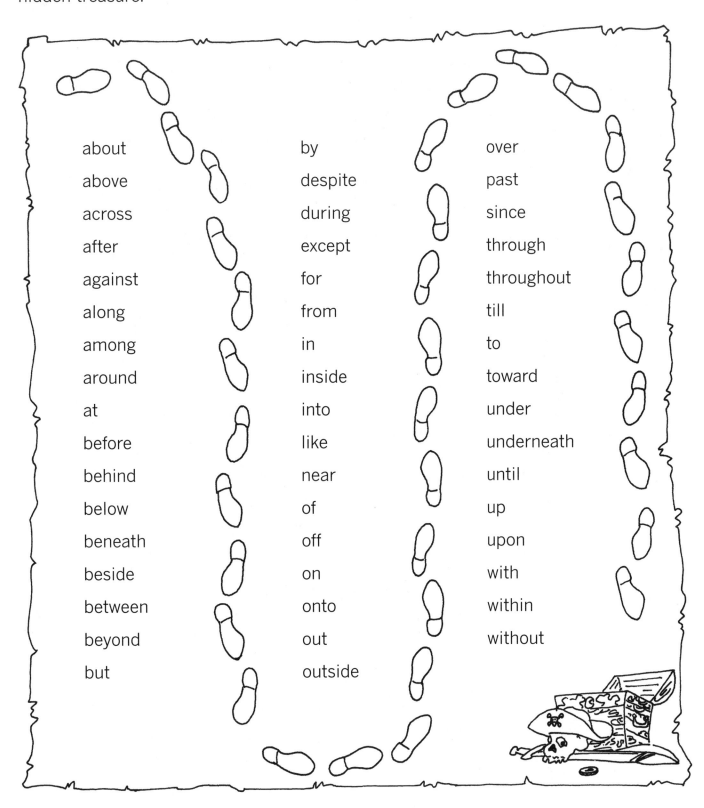

about	by	over
above	despite	past
across	during	since
after	except	through
against	for	throughout
along	from	till
among	in	to
around	inside	toward
at	into	under
before	like	underneath
behind	near	until
below	of	up
beneath	off	upon
beside	on	with
between	onto	within
beyond	out	without
but	outside	

How Many Homophones?

Standard

Apply knowledge of language structure, language conventions (e.g., spelling and punctuation), media techniques, figurative language, and genre to create, critique, and discuss print and nonprint texts.

Objective

Students will identify and use homophones in a creative and competitive game.

Students often confuse and misuse words that sound alike but have different meanings. These words are *homophones*. The following auditory/visual game will remind students of the specific meanings and correct usage of these confusing words.

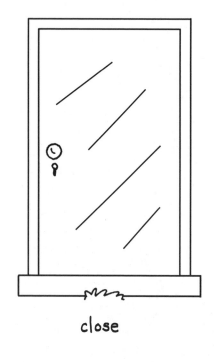

clothes

1. For this game, use the following homophones and any other homophones your students misuse. You may also find additional homophones listed online, such as at Educational Oasis: Homophones: *www.educationoasis.com/curriculum/Lang_Arts/ resources/homophones.htm: aloud, allowed; blue, blew; close, clothes; guessed, guest; pair, pear, pare; patience, patients; principal, principle; sail, sale; sent, scent, cent; sight, cite, site; so, sew, sow; stationary, stationery; there, their, they're; to, too, two.*

2. Divide the class into mixed-ability teams of four or five. Then review the differences between *homophones* (same sound), *homographs* (same spelling), and *homonyms* (same sound and spelling). For example: homophones *wait, weight*; homographs *tear* (crying), *tear* (rip); homonyms *bark* (tree cover), *bark* (dog sound).

3. Start the game by choosing a student from each team. Say a homophone, and have those students write a sentence on the board using all the related homophones and underline them. For example: *I **guessed** that the **guest** sitting next to me was famous.* Give each team a point for every sentence that makes sense and correctly uses the homophones. Continue with other students and homophones until everyone has had a turn. The team with the most points wins.

4. Conclude the activity by having students write sets of homophones and their meanings in their vocabulary journals.

close

The Note Passing Game

Standard

Employ a wide range of strategies while writing, and use different writing process elements appropriately to communicate with different audiences for a variety of purposes.

Objective

Students will practice writing and correcting each other's sentences.

Materials

writing paper
counters

This game is an excellent strategy for helping students become better proofreaders. When turning in papers, students often forget to carefully proofread their work; however, this game will serve as an effective reminder.

1. Review an anonymous corrected paper with the class. Point out simple mistakes that could have been avoided if it had been proofread carefully before it was turned in.

2. Give each student 15 counters (or tokens) and a sheet of writing paper. Post the following game rules on the board, and review them with the class:
   - No talking for the duration of the game.
   - All communication must be in the form of writing.
   - You may write any appropriate question or comment on your paper and then give it to a classmate.
   - The recipient should read the paper and respond in writing.
   - If the recipient of your note spots an error of any kind—grammatical, spelling, usage, punctuation, and so on—they may take one of your tokens.
   - If anyone catches you talking, they may take one of your tokens.
   - Once you are out of tokens, you are out of the game and must put your head down for the remainder of the activity or write quietly in your journal.
   - At the end of the game, the student with the most tokens wins.

3. Give students 15 minutes to complete the game. Monitor their progress, making sure they write and respond to each other appropriately. If students have disagreements about mistakes they find in the notes, step in as a mediator. Remind students to check their papers for mistakes before passing them to another student.

4. After the game, initiate a class discussion about the types of errors found. Ask students questions such as: *What seem to be the most common errors? How can you prevent making errors like this in the future?*

Ideas for More Differentiation

Post or distribute a list of commonly misspelled words, punctuation errors, and misused words to help students find the mistakes in their own and each other's work.

Extend the Activity

Use this approach throughout the year whenever you have a short paragraph or other writing assignment due. Give each student some tokens, and have partners trade papers and proofread each other's work.

What Are Euphemisms?

Standards

- Adjust the use of spoken, written, and visual language (e.g., conventions, style, vocabulary) to communicate effectively with a variety of audiences and for different purposes.

- Develop an understanding of and respect for diversity in language use, patterns, and dialects across cultures, ethnic groups, geographic regions, and social roles.

Strategies
Journaling

Brainstorming

Objective

Students will explore euphemisms in spoken and written language.

Materials

journals

This activity focuses on word choice, helping students understand the importance of using euphemistic synonyms when referring to delicate and sensitive issues.

1. Write words on the board that describe someone in a negative way (avoid offensive words), such as *lazy, fat, stupid, ugly*. Have students write in their journals about their experiences hearing those or other hurtful words. Encourage them to reflect on the feelings these words evoked.

2. Refer back to the words on the board, and have students brainstorm gentler words, such as *laid-back* instead of *lazy* or *heavy* instead of *fat*. List their suggestions on the board, crossing out the original words.

3. Explain that these gentler expressions are called *euphemisms*—inoffensive expressions used in place of offensive ones. They are used to avoid hurting people's feelings, to be more politically correct, or to make something sound better. For example: *used cars* for *pre-owned cars, toilet* for *restroom*.

This pre-owned car is a real gem!

4. Have students work in small groups to come up with more euphemisms for each word listed on the board or for other unacceptable words they have seen or heard. Invite volunteers to read their lists out loud.

Captain Capitalization

Strategy
Multiple intelligences

Standard

Apply knowledge of language structure, language conventions (e.g., spelling and punctuation), media techniques, figurative language, and genre to create, critique, and discuss print and nonprint texts.

Objective

Students will use their knowledge of capitalization and dialogue to create a comic strip.

Materials

sample comic strips from newspapers
paper to make comic strips
art supplies

Creating and sharing humorous comic strips is a natural motivator for students to learn proper language structure. In this activity, students practice using correct capitalization in direct quotations as they write and illustrate comic-book-style cartoons.

1. Choose four advanced learners to sit in different corners of the room and act as Capitalization Captains. Make sure these students have a thorough understanding of capitalization rules for writing dialogue.

2. Divide the rest of the class among the four captains, and give your experts ten to fifteen minutes to review with their group how to capitalize direct quotations. Provide captains with dialogue-rich text; or have them work with their group to write a dialogue using characters from a popular novel, television show, or movie.

3. After checking understanding of capitalization and how to write dialogue, invite students to work independently or with a partner to draw a comic strip that includes written dialogue. Provide them with paper and art supplies. You might also provide sample comic strips and access to computers that have clipart.

4. When they're finished, invite groups to exchange and read each other's comic strips. Display students' work on a bulletin board.

Ideas for More Differentiation

Give students comics from the Sunday paper or old comic books with the dialogue covered with paper or correction fluid or tape. Have students write their own dialogue for the pictures.

CHAPTER 4

Listening and Speaking

What Else Can It Be?

Standards
- Use spoken, written, and visual language to accomplish a purpose (e.g., for learning, enjoyment, persuasion, and the exchange of information).
- Adjust the use of spoken, written, and visual language (e.g., conventions, style, vocabulary) to communicate effectively with a variety of audiences and for different purposes.

Objective
Students will listen to and observe classmates describing and demonstrating new uses for common objects and then summarize and evaluate each presentation.

Materials
Presentation Evaluation reproducible
box of everyday objects
journals or writing paper

This activity opens the door to creative thinking as students devise and present new and original ways to use ordinary objects. It also encourages students to express their ideas clearly and completely, both visually and verbally.

1. Collect a variety of everyday objects (assorted school objects, household objects, tools, appliances, toys), and put them in a large box in the center of the classroom. Explain to students that they have been chosen to be renovation entrepreneurs and think of new, creative uses for the items in the box.

2. Have each student choose an object from the box. Give students a few minutes to jot down ideas about new ways to use the object. For example, a large serving bowl could become an ottoman to raise your feet beneath your desk. You might also have students brainstorm ideas with a partner.

3. Call on students to demonstrate and explain the new use for their chosen object. Remind them to speak clearly and completely,

Strategies
Presentation

Reflection after learning

maintain eye contact, and be persuasive about their innovative ideas. Tell audience members to listen carefully and jot down notes in their journals describing what they see and hear, noting the name of the speaker, and summarizing his or her ideas.

4. After the presentations, give each student several copies of the **Presentation Evaluation reproducible (page 79)**, and have students critique each presentation in sequence. Encourage them to refer to their notes to evaluate each speaker. (You may also choose to have students evaluate each speaker in turn directly after each presentation.) Collect the evaluations and save them for later distribution or for portfolios.

5. Conclude the activity by leading a class discussion about the presentations. Compare and contrast the different ideas and insights among the presentations and how each student utilized his or her prior knowledge to come up with new ideas.

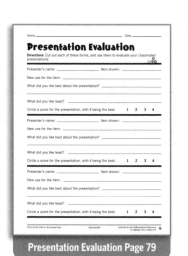

Presentation Evaluation Page 79

Ideas for More Differentiation

Invite students with a high degree of mastery to invent their own gadget, draw a design or make a model of it, and present a sales pitch to potential investors or buyers.

Name _____ Date _____

Presentation Evaluation

Directions: Cut out each of these forms, and use them to evaluate your classmates' presentations.

Presenter's name: _____ Item shown: _____

New use for the item: _____

What did you like best about the presentation? _____

_____

What did you like least? _____

Circle a score for the presentation, with 4 being the best:　　**1　　2　　3　　4**

Presenter's name: _____ Item shown: _____

New use for the item: _____

What did you like best about the presentation? _____

_____

What did you like least? _____

Circle a score for the presentation, with 4 being the best:　　**1　　2　　3　　4**

Presenter's name: _____ Item shown: _____

New use for the item: _____

What did you like best about the presentation? _____

_____

What did you like least? _____

Circle a score for the presentation, with 4 being the best:　　**1　　2　　3　　4**

Stand Up for Capitals

Strategies

Focus activity

Multiple intelligences

Standard

Apply knowledge of language structure, language conventions (e.g., spelling and punctuation), media techniques, figurative language, and genre to create, critique, and discuss print and nonprint texts.

Objective

Students will play a game to identify words that should be capitalized in a reading passage.

Materials

dialogue-rich passage from a novel or magazine

This activity will undoubtedly keep your class on their toes as they listen for and identify correct usage of capitalization. Students will laugh at themselves and each other as they stand up and sit down, trying to keep up with the reading.

1. Choose a dialogue-rich passage from a novel or magazine. Explain to students that they should stand up every time they hear you read a word that should be capitalized. (You might also want to mention an alternative assignment for students who are tempted to act too silly or inappropriately.)

2. Have the class stand up as a whole group each time they hear you read a word that should be capitalized. Or, play an elimination game in which students are eliminated if they stand up at the wrong time, leaving one final student as the winner.

3. Start off slowly, giving students time to think carefully before deciding whether or not to stand. Then increase the pace, challenging them to decide more quickly.

4. Keep track of any difficulties students experience identifying correct usage of capitalization. Review those concepts with students afterward or in later lessons.

Ideas for More Differentiation

For beginning mastery students or those with difficulty following auditory lessons, give them a copy of the text (without capitals) so they can follow along as you read.

Class Introductions

Standard

Use spoken, written, and visual language to accomplish a purpose (e.g., for learning, enjoyment, persuasion, and the exchange of information).

Objective

Students will interview classmates and give a speech about them.

Materials

Student Interview reproducible
video of a speech (optional)
tape recorders (optional)

Strategies
Think-Pair-Share

Authentic task

In this activity, students gain a greater understanding of the importance of proper public introductions and the power of being a good speaker.

1. Invite students to share their thoughts about what makes a good speech and a good speaker. If possible, show a video of a speech (such as Martin Luther King Jr.'s "I Have a Dream" speech), and have students point out the impressive parts.

2. Tell students that they will give a speech about a very important topic: each other. You may have them simply introduce a classmate, or they may present the person as a pitch for a specific job or a political campaign (such as presenting political candidates for president).

3. Assign partners, or have students choose their own. Distribute copies of the **Student Interview reproducible (page 82)**, and review it with ▶ the class. Invite students to suggest other questions to add.

4. Provide time for students to interview their partners. Encourage them to add any additional questions or answers that may arise. After they complete their interview, instruct students to write and practice a five-minute speech introducing their partner.

5. Invite students to present their speeches. Remind the audience to be respectful listeners and to applaud at the end of each speech.

Ideas for More Differentiation

Encourage students to record their interviews so they can review them and listen for important details they overlooked in their notes. You might also allow students to refer to their notes when giving their speech.

Student Interview Page 82

Student Interview

Directions: Gather information for your speech. Think about the questions you would like to ask your partner. Write them down before you begin your interview. Here's a list to get you started. Add more questions, and then conduct your interview. You might also tape-record the interview so you can listen to it later.

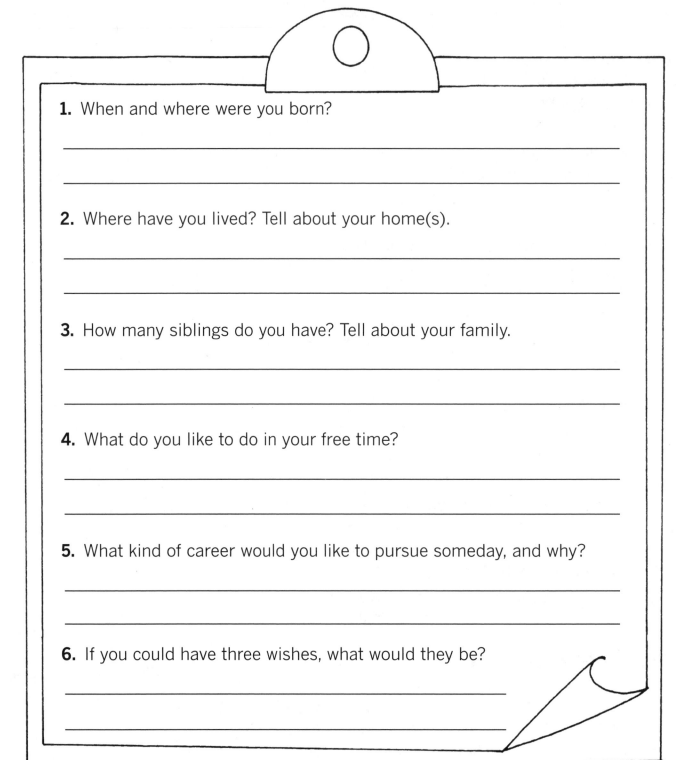

1. When and where were you born?

_____

_____

2. Where have you lived? Tell about your home(s).

_____

_____

3. How many siblings do you have? Tell about your family.

_____

_____

4. What do you like to do in your free time?

_____

_____

5. What kind of career would you like to pursue someday, and why?

_____

_____

6. If you could have three wishes, what would they be?

_____

_____

Mini Mysteries

Standards

- Participate as knowledgeable, reflective, creative, and critical members of a variety of literacy communities.

- Use spoken, written, and visual language to accomplish a purpose (e.g., for learning, enjoyment, persuasion, and the exchange of information).

Objective

Students will use their listening skills and deductive reasoning to solve mini mysteries.

Materials

Mini Mystery reproducible
collection of mini mysteries

The intrigue of a good mystery is a natural attention-grabber for middle-grade learners, especially when it is read aloud dramatically. Your students will be on the edge of their seats as they try to anticipate and predict what happens next, motivating them to be both attentive listeners and deductive problem-solvers.

1. Gather a collection of mini mysteries from books and online resources. Preread them, and choose one that includes a lot of clues and plot twists.

2. Give each student a copy of the **Mini Mystery reproducible (page 85)**, and review the directions with students. Point out that you will stop at five different places in the mystery to allow the class to record clues and predictions about what happens next. Emphasize the importance of listening carefully.

3. Read the mystery aloud, stopping at five different critical points in the plot. At each pause, give students a few minutes to write down clues and their predictions in one of the five magnifying glasses on the Mini Mystery reproducible.

4. At the end of the story, have students write the solution to the mystery and draw a star next to their correct predictions.

5. Invite volunteers to share their results and relate which of their predictions were correct. Encourage students to compare and discuss the different clues and explain how those clues could have been misleading or misinterpreted.

Mini Mystery Page 85

6. Repeat the activity with another mystery, or have partners read mysteries to each other. Have them complete a reproducible for every mystery they read.

Ideas for More Differentiation

For visual learners or those who have difficulty with auditory learning, provide a copy of the story to follow along as you read aloud. You might also invite your bodily/kinesthetic learners to role-play and reenact the mystery for the class. You may have performers hold up word cards and clue cards to help English Language Learners and other students needing extra support.

Extend the Activity

- Repeat this activity during transition times, or read aloud a mystery once a week.

- Invite students to write their own mini mystery and challenge their classmates to solve it.

Name _____   Date _____

Mini Mystery

Directions: Are you an expert sleuth? Write clues and predictions in each magnifying glass as you follow the storyline. After the solution is revealed, draw a star next to each correct prediction.

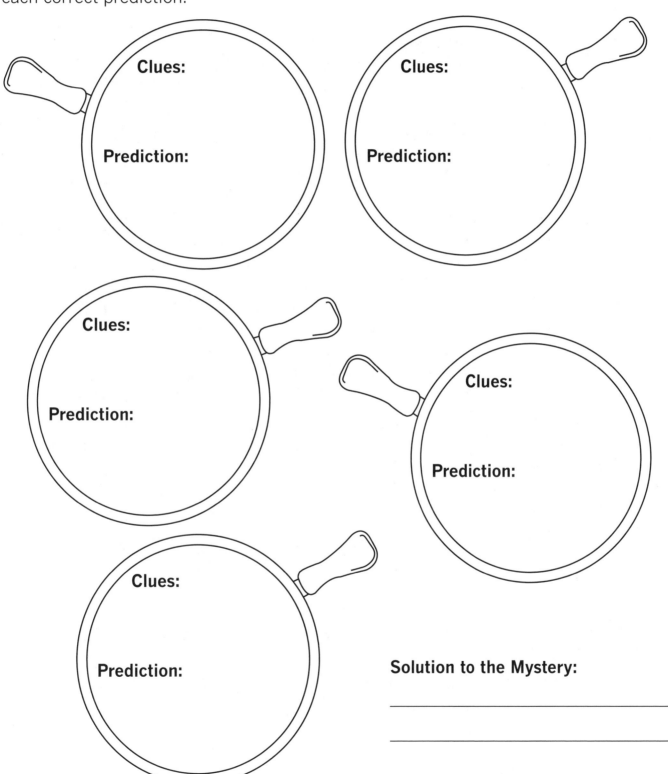

Clues:

Prediction:

Clues:

Prediction:

Clues:

Prediction:

Clues:

Prediction:

Clues:

Prediction:

Solution to the Mystery:

_____

_____

Filter Out the Fillers

Strategies

Game

Presentation

Standard
Adjust the use of spoken, written, and visual language (e.g., conventions, style, vocabulary) to communicate effectively with a variety of audiences and for different purposes.

Objective
Students will adjust their spoken language to exclude fillers such as *um, uh,* and *like.*

Materials
Topic Cards reproducible
Speech Organizer reproducible
Speaker Evaluation Forms reproducible
scissors
paper bag
copy of Lincoln's "Gettysburg Address" or other well-known speech

Being able to speak fluently and confidently without the use of slang or other filler words is a struggle for most teenagers. This activity will help students become more aware of their speech patterns and become better communicators.

Topic Cards Page 88

1. In advance, cut apart the **Topic Cards reproducible (page 88)**, and put the cards in a paper bag. Or, use your own topics written on separate index cards.

2. Ask students to list situations in which being an articulate speaker is important, such as in a courtroom, as part of a sales presentation, or during a political campaign.

3. Then ask students to list words that speakers inadvertently use as fillers when they're trying to collect their thoughts during a speech, such as *um, uh, like,* or *you know.* Explain that when these fillers are used in excess, they can be very distracting to an audience and dilute the effectiveness and impact of a speech.

4. Demonstrate by reading aloud a well-known speech, such as Lincoln's "Gettysburg Address," and include some fillers (such as *um, uh, like,* and *you know*). Then reread it without the fillers. Invite students to share their thoughts about the two different

versions. (You may download a copy of the "Gettysburg Address" from the Internet.)

5. Ask students to suggest ways to avoid using fillers. For example: *Pause and take a breath; slow down; practice speaking without using any fillers*. Then announce to the class that they will be playing a game to help them improve their public-speaking skills. The object of the game is to give a one-minute, impromptu speech about a chosen topic without using any fillers.

6. Have students each choose a topic card from the bag and spend a few minutes brainstorming ideas about what they are going to say about it. Give them the option of filling out a **Speech Organizer reproducible (page 89)**. ▶

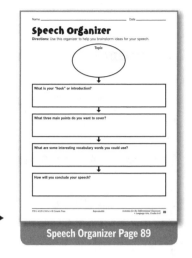

Speech Organizer Page 89

7. Distribute several copies of the **Speaker Evaluation Forms reproducible (page 90)** to each student, and review the directions with the class. Explain that they should fill out a form for each speaker. ▶

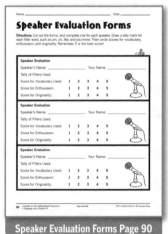

Speaker Evaluation Forms Page 90

8. Call on students at random to give their impromptu speeches. (You might write their names on strips of paper and then draw the strips to decide on the order.) Remind classmates to listen carefully and mark each evaluation form accordingly.

9. At the end of class, collect the evaluation forms. Determine each student's overall score by adding the circled scores and subtracting the number of tallies. Announce the winner the following day.

Ideas for More Differentiation

If some students feel uncomfortable about giving an impromptu speech, allow them to use their Speech Organizer, stand at their desk, or work with a partner.

Extend the Activity

Repeat this game periodically throughout the year, or have students take turns daily or weekly giving impromptu speeches at the beginning or end of class.

Topic Cards

How to be a good customer	How to take effective notes	Talk about a famous U.S. president
How to behave in a restaurant	How to exercise properly	Talk about the meaning of friendship
How to make pancakes	How to braid hair	Talk about proper nutrition
Talk about your best friend	How to paint your toenails	Talk about your idol or hero
How to make a salad	How to manage your money	Talk about your family
How to study for a test	How to bathe a dog or cat	Talk about your career ambitions
How to apply for a job	How to clean your room	Talk about your favorite holiday
How to be a good friend	Talk about your favorite book or movie	Talk about ways to save the environment

978-1-4129-5343-6 • © Corwin Press

Speech Organizer

Directions: Use this organizer to help you brainstorm ideas for your speech.

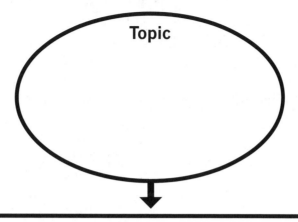

Topic

What is your hook or introduction?

What three main points do you want to cover?

What are some interesting vocabulary words you could use?

How will you conclude your speech?

Name _____ Date _____

Speaker Evaluation Forms

Directions: Cut out the forms, and complete one for each speaker. Draw a tally mark for each filler word, such as *um, uh, like,* and *you know.* Then circle scores for vocabulary, enthusiasm, and originality. Remember, 5 is the best score!

Speaker Evaluation

Speaker's Name: _____   Your Name: _____

Tally of Fillers Used:

Score for Vocabulary Used:	1	2	3	4	5
Score for Enthusiasm:	1	2	3	4	5
Score for Originality:	1	2	3	4	5

Speaker Evaluation

Speaker's Name: _____   Your Name: _____

Tally of Fillers Used:

Score for Vocabulary Used:	1	2	3	4	5
Score for Enthusiasm:	1	2	3	4	5
Score for Originality:	1	2	3	4	5

Speaker Evaluation

Speaker's Name: _____   Your Name: _____

Tally of Fillers Used:

Score for Vocabulary Used:	1	2	3	4	5
Score for Enthusiasm:	1	2	3	4	5
Score for Originality:	1	2	3	4	5

Reproducible   978-1-4129-5343-6 • © Corwin Press

Speaking of . . .

Standards

- Conduct research on issues and interests by generating ideas and questions and posing problems. Gather, evaluate, and synthesize data from a variety of sources (e.g., print and nonprint texts, artifacts, people) to communicate their discoveries in ways that suit the purpose and audience.

- Use spoken, written, and visual language to accomplish a purpose (e.g., for learning, enjoyment, persuasion, and the exchange of information).

Objective

Students will organize and present a tribute speech in honor of a heroic individual.

Materials

Tribute Research reproducible
Certificate of Appreciation reproducible
Tribute Reviews reproducible
copy of Ronald Regan's speech "Address to the Nation on the Challenger Disaster"
art supplies

This activity takes writing out of the classroom and into the real world. By writing a tribute to honor people they admire and respect, students learn the art of persuasive writing and discover what motivates ordinary people to accomplish extraordinary things.

1. Explain to students that they will be giving a tribute speech in honor of someone they respect and admire. Ask them to share what they know about a tribute speech. Explain that a tribute speech is given to honor a person's achievements; it is different from a simple biographical speech in that its purpose is to instill a sense of admiration about that person.

2. Share Ronald Regan's speech "Address to the Nation on the Challenger Disaster." (You can find videos of the speech at many libraries or the transcript at the Ronald Reagan Presidential Library and Foundation Web site: *http://www.reaganfoundation.org/reagan/speeches/challenger.asp.*) Invite students to share their thoughts and feelings about the speech.

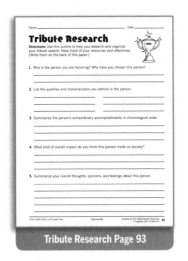

Tribute Research Page 93

Certificate of Appreciation Page 94

3. Ask students to think of three people they would like to honor in a tribute speech. They may choose people from history, the news, their neighborhood, or their circle of family and friends. Have them write their three choices and the reasons for those choices on a sheet of paper and circle their favorite choice. (You might want to give students a day or two to think about and complete this assignment.)

4. Collect and review students' choices to see if everyone has chosen different people. If not, ask those students to select one of their other two choices. Then set up a schedule for students to give their speeches, listing the name of each speaker, the person being honored, and the day and time set aside for that speech.

5. Give students time in class to research information about their honorees and write their tribute speeches. Give them the option of using the **Tribute Research reproducible (page 93)** to organize their speeches. Encourage students to practice their speeches in front of friends and family members.

6. Have students make a certificate of appreciation for the person they are honoring. They may use the **Certificate of Appreciation reproducible (page 94)** or make their own. Encourage students to use visuals or make a poster to display during their speech.

7. Invite students to present their speeches to the class. (You might also invite parents and/or other classes to hear the presentations.) To encourage active listening, have audience members fill out copies of the **Tribute Reviews reproducible (page 95)**, noting what they liked about each presentation.

Name _____ Date _____

Tribute Research

Directions: Use this outline to help you research and organize your tribute speech. Keep track of your resources and references. (Write them on the back of this paper.)

1. Who is the person you are honoring? Why have you chosen this person?

_____

_____

2. List the qualities and characteristics you admire in the person.

_____   _____

_____   _____

_____   _____

3. Summarize the person's extraordinary accomplishments in chronological order.

_____

_____

_____

4. What kind of overall impact do you think this person made on society?

_____

_____

_____

5. Summarize your overall thoughts, opinions, and feelings about this person.

_____

_____

_____

_____

Name _____ Date _____

Certificate of Appreciation

Certificate of Appreciation

In honor of _____ for your important contributions to society.

We are honoring you for _____

Awarded on _____ (Date)

Reproducible

978-1-4129-5343-6 • © Corwin Press

Tribute Reviews

Directions: Cut out the forms, and write your thoughts and opinions about each tribute speech.

Speaker's name: _____

Person honored: _____

Your impressions of the tribute:

_____

_____

_____

Speaker's name: _____

Person honored: _____

Your impressions of the tribute:

_____

_____

_____

Speaker's name: _____

Person honored: _____

Your impressions of the tribute:

_____

_____

_____

References

Gregory, G. H., & Chapman, C. (2002). *Differentiated instructional strategies: One size doesn't fit all, second edition.* Thousand Oaks, CA: Corwin Press.

National Council for the Social Studies. (2002). *Expectations of excellence: Curriculum standards for social studies.* Silver Spring, MD: National Council for the Social Studies (NCSS).

National Council of Teachers of English and International Reading Association. (1996). *Standards for the English language arts.* Urbana, IL: National Council of Teachers of English (NCTE).

National Council of Teachers of Mathematics. (2005). *Principles and standards for school mathematics.* Reston, VA: National Council of Teachers of Mathematics (NCTM).

National Research Council. (2005). *National science education standards.* Washington, DC: National Academy Press.

Robb, K. (n.d.). *Book report list one.* Retrieved September 17, 2006, from the TeachNet.com Web site: http://www.teachnet.com/lesson/langarts/reading/bookreps1.html.

Source Watch: A Project of the Center for Media & Democracy. (n.d.). *Propaganda techniques.* Retrieved September 17, 2006, from http://www.sourcewatch.org/index.php?title=Propagandatechniques.

Wikipedia: The Free Encyclopedia. (n.d.). *Types of propaganda.* Retrieved September 20, 2006, from http://en.wikipedia.org/wiki/Propaganda#Types of Propaganda.